Bharat Rochlin has studied palmistry and tarot and has given readings for over 20 years. He is one of the most perceptive and skilled practitioners today. Bharat lives in south India and the Himalayas, with occasional visits to the West.

PALMISTRY

A Comprehensive and Reflective Guide
for the Study and Practice of Palmistry

BHARAT ROCHLIN

Watkins Publishing
London

This edition published in the UK in 2003 by
Watkins Publishing, 20 Bloomsbury Street, London, WC1B 3QA
www.watkinspublishing.com

Cover design by Echelon Design
Cover illustration by Jane Adams
Hand illustrations by Jane Adams, assisted by Lilian Vajtho
Designed and typeset by Echelon Design, Wimborne
Printed and bound in Great Britain by J. H. Haynes & Co., Sparkford

British Library Cataloguing in Publication data available

Library of Congress Cataloguing in Publication data available

ISBN 1 84293 067 2

For all and everyone

CONTENTS

LIST OF FIGURES

ACKNOWLEDGEMENTS

I am profoundly grateful to existence in the form of Ma Prem Sona, who initiated me into the esoteric mysteries; to Dhanyam, who unknowingly turned me on to palmistry; and to Papaji for his boon of palmistry.

I am indebted to every palmist, to every palmistry book and to every hand I've ever read and every pair of eyes I've looked into.

I want to thank Ishi and Kumari, who showed up by chance in the far reaches of the Himalayas with a laptop, which I used to write this book.

I also want to thank Chris Boys and the staff at Watkins Publishing for their much needed input, Paula Marvelly for introducing me to Watkins, and a big thank-you to them for publishing this book.

PREFACE

Welcome to the world of palmistry, and perhaps the beginning of a journey into the expanding awareness of 'who you are' with regard to the mind-body-personality mechanism that you possess.

It is fun to learn the meanings of lines and correlate them with your traits and qualities and those of others. It is always good to learn more about your own self, enabling you to have a greater understanding of your inner mechanisms. Understanding the systems involved can be very useful, even though you might not be able to change your ways.

Giving a reading and meeting with another with the intent to look within is both fascinating for you and extremely helpful for the person you are guiding.

Fortune telling is a part of palmistry and can be valuable in making certain decisions. However, because I believe that all is predestined, that 'the story' has already been told, I tend to keep away from fortune telling. But, of course, you can do as you like with the information I give you.

Each chapter has clear illustrations of everything described – right there at your fingertips!

I hope you will enjoy palmistry and find it an interesting skill to learn.

Good luck!

INTRODUCTION

This book contains the knowledge accumulated from my study and practice of palmistry over the last 20 years. It is not complete, but there is a system to it, and a basis of moving from logic to intuition and from intuition to logic.

I present only the information I use and know to be true. I do not offer anything that has not been verified by observation. So please do not expect a textbook. I am expressing a fragment of a teaching that you can use to build your own store of knowledge. However, there is more than enough information to enable you to make a proper reading.

You will find interpretations here that you will not discover in any other palmistry book. These have come to me over the years and I am sure they are correct.

It is my conclusion that nearly everything can be seen in the lines and shapes of the hands. The big exception for me is the indication of children in the subject's hand. I've yet to find any accurate information about children in the hand.

How I see and interpret the lines is unique. Every palmist interprets and sees something according to his viewpoint and the subculture he associates with. No one ever sees the whole picture, since in reality truth is beyond our limited understanding. It is always a look through the peephole, and even if it is a large peephole, perception is still limited. *The key to the information in the hand is the palmist's knowledge and his skill at interpreting the lines and shape of the hand.*

The lines of the palm are not stagnant or fixed. They are constantly changing and reforming. The mounts become bigger and smaller depending on the momentary energy levels. If the nerves leading to the palm are cut, the lines disappear. The lines are not present just because that is the way the hand folds; rather, the lines of the palm are alive and vibrant in their own right. They can best be described as a biocomputer readout of energy patterns. The headline represents the mental body, the heartline the emotional body, and the lifeline the general vitality and movement of overall energy. This biocomputer readout covers all our mental, emotional, psychological and spiritual channels, and even shows past-life tendencies and issues. Palmistry is, in fact, very similar to astrology. A palmistry reading should give the same results as an astrology reading, only reached by looking through a different window.

My approach to palmistry is to examine the mental, emotional, psychological and spiritual make-up of subjects as indicated by the lines and shape of their hands. This approach helps them to understand tendencies and habits; to see blocks, shortcomings, talents and advantages; and to see where they are in terms of enlightenment.

I look for tendencies and patterns, how they react in certain situations, what tools and talents they have and what tools they lack. All this helps them to understand their nature and is thus very valuable.

When you are studying and reading this book, you will notice that I make many references to past lives. Now, for me, past lives are not a belief but knowledge and recognition of an aspect of reality. I've come to realise, however, that it is difficult to see the whole picture or have a full understanding of past lives. Past lives do exist but perhaps not exactly in the way they are presently thought of. Still, I've had very clear visions and memories of past lives, and people I trust absolutely have had similar experiences and have even gone to graves and areas where they lived before. In my life I have been in places where I knew everything about them and yet had never been there before.

It is my understanding that life itself is a dream, and our past lives are dreams which are incorporated into the dreams we are having now.

If you are too much of a rationalist then translate what I say about past lives into genetics. Perhaps that can open a door for you. It could be that we absorb collective dreams at birth, or even before – most often the dreams and memories of our parents. Whether we actually lived a particular memory of a past life has to be determined. I am certain that some of my past memories come from the memories of my father.

The first five chapters of this book cover the nomenclature and meanings of the lines, mounts and hand shapes. In the final chapter I discuss how to give a reading and how to make interpretations.

Step one is to learn the nomenclature and the meanings of the lines, mounts and shapes of the hand. The next step is to investigate whether the meanings given are true. This investigation can take up to seven to ten years. You cannot usually be called a master palmist before completing seven years of study. This does not mean that you cannot give a reading – and a good one – before that time. In general, though, you need this amount of time to gain sufficient mastery. But don't get discouraged; you can give a reading even after a very short time and with a small amount of knowledge. It will be a limited reading, but still a helpful one. As your knowledge increases, the scope of the reading will increase. So don't worry about learning everything at once. For example, it took me years before I could include mounts in my readings. At first, I couldn't recognise the mounts and see their differences. By and by, I began to be able to recognise the mounts and their relationships to each other. I could then include the meanings of the mounts in my readings.

Learning the meanings of the lines is like learning the meaning of words. Once the meanings of the words are known, then sentences can be put together to form an interpretation. Usually this sentence is more than the sum of the words. These words can also be seen as signposts or pieces of a puzzle which when put together tell a story.

The first palm to read is your own. Reading your own palm is most interesting and a very good way to learn. This interest will never stop, especially when there are changes in the lines and shape of the hands. Since you know your own characteristics, it is easy to see if the meaning of a line is correct. This will give you a good basis for trusting the meaning of the lines.

Before I became a palmist, I was a Tarot card reader. However, while watching a man reading palms at a party I became jealous of his popularity and decided to learn palmistry as well. I bought some books and then started to analyse my own hand. I was profoundly impressed how accurate the meanings of the lines were. So from a silly reason to start studying palmistry I became seriously interested and embarked on a systematic study of it.

Even if you never give a reading, it is useful to know palmistry just for the understanding it will give you regarding your mind-body-personality.

Whatever brings you here doesn't matter. Whatever the reason, you can make a good study of palmistry and gain something from it. Take your time, go slowly, read all the books, look at your own palm and the palms of others. Don't look for results and one day you will be surprised that you are able to read palms.

I have spontaneously put together a short list of what I can tell from the palm. It is not complete but it will give you a good idea of what palmistry can reveal. I find palmistry to be quite accurate in these particular areas. The only limitation is the palmist's level of intuition and intelligence.

I can tell from the palm:

- past-life tendencies, including issues reoccurring from other lives
- whether a child was wanted or not and how much love was present at conception
- the love of the mother
- the role of the father
- stability and development in childhood
- intelligence, and the ability to use it
- emotional strength and the ability to love deeply
- the effect of childhood, as shown in the shape of the fingers
- weakness in physical organs and predisposition to disease
- degree of independence, recklessness or caution
- the state of the life force, strong or weak, and when each occurs
- greed and ambition
- relationship with others
- creativity and love of art
- luck
- psychic influences

- challenges in life
- predisposition to depression
- honesty, and whether a person lives in a dream world
- abilities to direct and organise and manifest in life
- influxes and losses of life force
- mid-life crises
- how the soul enters the body
- passion of life-force energy
- tendency to laziness
- how loving and giving a person is
- spontaneity and degree of flexibility or inflexibility
- confidence and self-worth
- dominating life issues
- and, of course, the usual things about the head line, life line and heart line

Details on all these points can be found within the book.

THE LINES, MOUNTS AND FINGERS

On the following pages are five illustrations showing:

I   primary lines
II secondary lines
III names of mounts
IV meaning of mounts
V   active and passive hands

It is best to memorise everything here before continuing. It will make learning a lot easier.

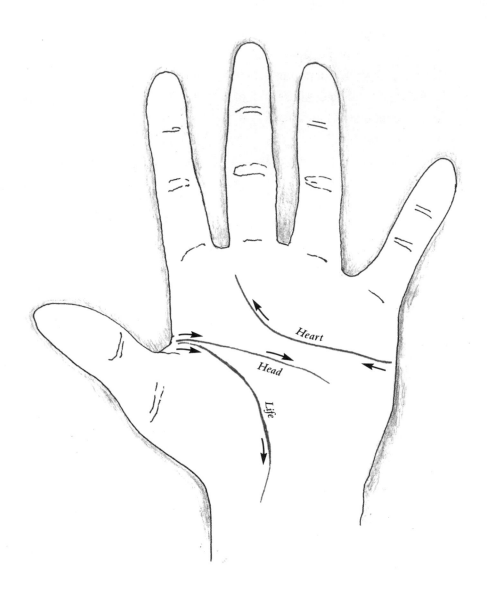

Fig. I Primary Lines

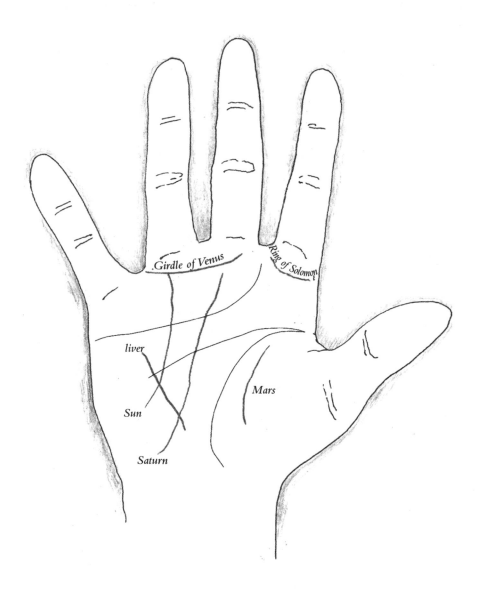

Fig. II Secondary Lines

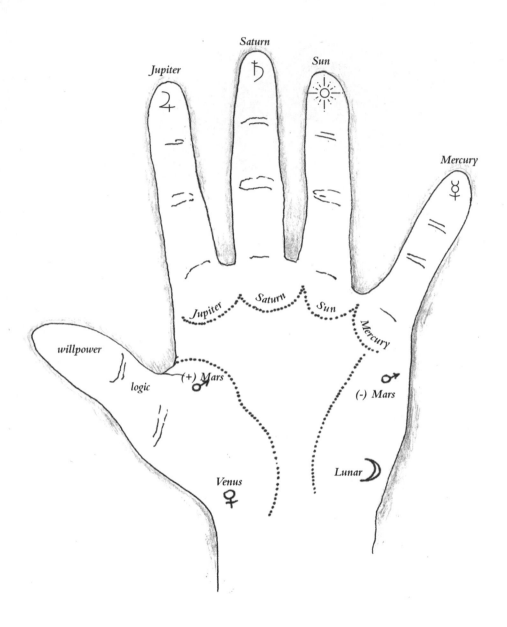

Fig. III Names of Mounts

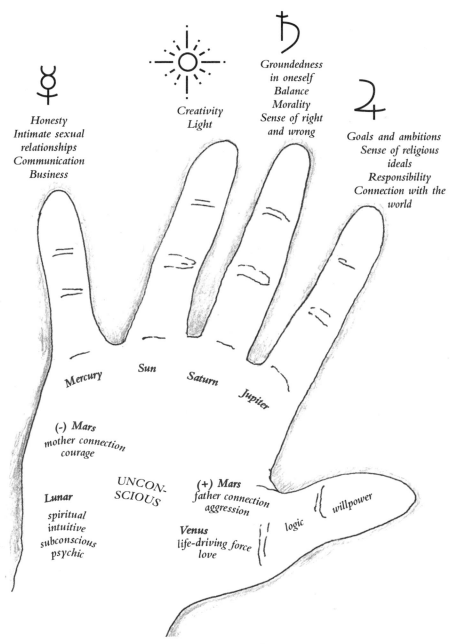

Honesty
Intimate sexual
relationships
Communication
Business

Creativity
Light

Groundedness
in oneself
Balance
Morality
Sense of right
and wrong

Goals and ambitions
Sense of religious
ideals
Responsibility
Connection with the
world

Mercury

Sun

Saturn

Jupiter

(-) Mars
mother connection
courage

UNCON-
SCIOUS

(+) Mars
father connection
aggression

willpower

Lunar

spiritual
intuitive
subconscious
psychic

logic

Venus
life-driving force
love

Fig. IV Meaning of Mounts

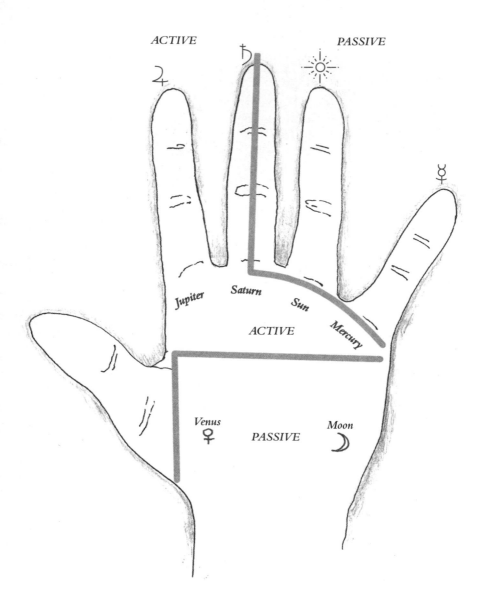

Fig. V Active and Passive Hands

These diagrams are all hand drawn and very idealised. I have found that it is easier to learn from such drawings than from photographs. Photographs can be confusing, even for an experienced palmist. A photograph is almost always a distorted representation, and even when it is not can pick up only 60 per cent of what is in the hand.

When you begin to look at hands, don't expect them to always have clear-cut lines as shown in the diagrams. However, you will be surprised how often the examples given are exactly like those you will find in the hands.

The first four diagrams are self-explanatory, but the fifth needs some explanation. The hand can be divided into active and passive areas. The top half of the palm, which includes the mount of Jupiter, Saturn, Sun and Mercury, is active. In the bottom half, the moon is passive, and the mount of Venus has a passive and active function. Venus is active because it is connected to the thumb and moves with it, and the thumb is active. Venus is passive because it is the reservoir of energy and life force, available on many levels.

The fingers can be active or passive. Jupiter is active. Saturn is active/ passive (which is why Saturn deals with balance). Sun and Mercury are passive.

The hand can be predominantly active or passive. If the bottom half of the palm predominates, that person is more likely to be centred in the passive areas of emotions, intuition and seeing in the 'inner world'. If the upper, active half is predominant, a person will be more focused on the outer world and manifesting therein.

The following chapters deal with all these points in detail.

Chapter 1

THE HAND:
PHYSICAL ASPECTS

The hands are one of our basic means of contact with the physical and sub-physical worlds. Can you imagine what life would be like without them? It is no wonder then that there is a direct correlation between the shape of the hand and how a person interacts with the world, and how a person interacts with the world influences the temperament of the person and vice versa.

The length and size of the thumb, palm and fingers determines to a large degree how easy it is 'to grab the world', so to speak. Therefore, in general, larger hands with a long thumb and fingers are more capable, simply because they are physically able to grab more.

The classification I present here is general. I start with the elementary hand and end with the artistic/refined hand. Everything in between I call the average shape.

The elementary and artistic hand shapes have a very distinct look and are easy to recognise. Within the average shape there are four basic hand types, the high- or low-set thumb, and the square or rectangular palm.

Slightly rectangular palms are the most common hand type. Square palms are generally associated with a person who is practical, careful, cautious and conservative, with a tendency towards conformity. These characteristics are very general, because often other aspects can greatly modify them. I find people with square palms tend to have a more 'mental' approach to life.

Generally, big hands and fingers belong to people capable of physical action, while people with small hands with small fingers and thumbs are usually less capable of physical action. Larger hands tend to belong to more earthy types who are able to do physical work.

In the hand there can be varying degrees of vitality and strength, and these qualities can vary day by day. If the hand is soft, some laziness is present. Firm hands are more energetic. Someone with soft hands can still be a doer. It depends on the strength of the lines and the strength of the thumb. The opposite can be true with firm hands; when lines and thumb are affected, the person can be lazy.

The basic shape of the hand gives information about capability and shows which of the elements is predominant: earth, fire, water or air.

Often I find a hand is a predominant mixture of fire and water or fire and earth, with minor amounts of the other elements.

The above classification is the result of my practical observation of hand shapes. It is not complete but empirical. Many palmistry books tend to overemphasise hand shapes, which I feel leads to confusion. My classification is simple and short and helps to demystify hand shapes.

Hand shapes are important in themselves, *but the influence of lines and other factors can and does so greatly modify the meaning of the hand shape that in practical terms the basic shape of the hand has only a minor influence upon the mind-body mechanism.*

BASIC HAND SHAPES

Elementary hand

The elementary hand is very distinct and is easy to recognise. The palm is broad and the fingers thick. The lines are simple and strong, without many secondary and influence lines. Every hand has a look and feel to it. The elementary hand does not look refined, nor does it give a feeling of refinement. Usually this is the hand of simple people who are physical workers, farmers, etc. Life for them is seen in terms of black and white, and emotions are basic and strong. The form of the hand is geared for manual, strong, physical work. The temperament of this hand is of the earth and it is considered an 'Earth hand'.

As the mind-body-personality evolves, normally the soul incarnates with a more developed hand that has a higher capacity to handle the increase in energy input. However, sometimes the lines in an elementary hand show some, or even a large, degree of development. The possessors of this hand are in most cases not very refined – they retain their elementary nature but their intelligence and outlook can be very broad (I know college professors with an elementary hand).

Very often possessors of this hand have problems handling a large amount of energy input because basically the elementary hand is not made for high energy flow. The circuits can burn out or most often shut down. Anger and physical breakdown are problems when overload occurs. On the plus side, these individuals can be very loving in such a simple and endearing way and it is very beautiful to be with them.

Artistic/sensitive hand

On the other side of the elementary hand is the artistic or sensitive hand. This is a fine, sensitive, tapering hand, and again it is very easy to recognise. Usually there is refinement and extreme sensitivity, as well as something ethereal about the person. This hand is not very common.

This hand contains the element air and is known as an 'Air hand'.

The refinement of this hand can result in both negative and positive qualities. The tapering shape of the hand increases its ability to absorb energy from the environment, thereby increasing the sensitivity of the person. Increased sensitivity is a positive quality when sensitivity is needed – when a person is engaging in artistic endeavours, for example – but is also a negative quality because it does not provide enough of a buffer to protect the person from incoming energy. A person with artistic hands is usually highly strung and must be treated with caution. What would be a normal flow of energy for most people can be excessive for a person with artistic hands.

Average hand

Between the elementary and the artistic hand lies the basic average hand. This hand is the most prevalent and the one you will see normally. There are many variations of the basic average hand. The fingers can be long, short or of equal length to the palm; the palm can be square or rectangular; the thumb can be high or low set, and the thumb can also be long or short.

The best way to measure is with a ruler, as shown in *fig. 1.1.*

Long fingers
Long fingers indicate an ability to look at and enjoy the details of projects and life. When combined with a good thumb, dexterity will be present. Concert pianists and film-makers usually have long fingers.

Short fingers
Short fingers mean less concern for detail. Interest is more on getting to the end rather than dwelling on the details. People with short fingers are more impulsive. I find that most people have short fingers in relationship to the palm.

Palm and fingers equal
Fingers and palms of equal length denote average, balanced intelligence.

Wide palm and short fingers
This hand contains the element of fire and is known as the 'Fire hand'. It is an active hand. People with this hand have much energy for creating and organising. However, they can burn out or, if they lose their passion, give up. These types can have radical Saturn Returns and changes of life. (Saturn Returns refer to the time when the planet Saturn completes its revolution around the Sun and comes to the position in the zodiac it occupied at the time of a person's birth. Saturn revolves around the Sun every 28 years. The time of Saturn Return is associated with a period of profound life changes and lessons.)

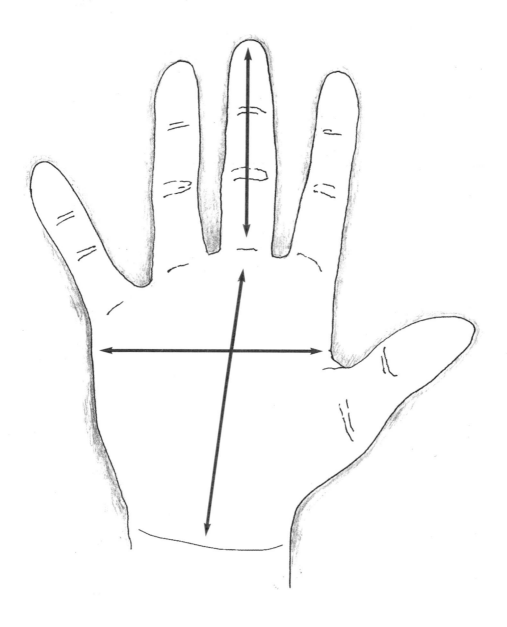

Fig. 1.1 Measuring the Palm

Long palm with either short or long fingers

This hand contains the element water and is known as the 'Water hand'. It is considered passive since a person with this hand is focused more on the intuitive and emotional side and lives more in the inner world. This is because the area of the passive mounts of Venus and Lunar is greater than the active mount area under the fingers.

MOUNTS

There are in the hand distinct risings called mounts. *See figs. III and IV* on pages xxii and xxiii. These mounts are located directly beneath each finger and cover most of the palm. In practical terms consider the whole area under each finger as a mount; on the palm, the left and right sides can usually be easily defined as mounts. Mounts contain bundles of nerve fibres which the fingers and the palm use in order to operate. A mount can be big or small, developed or not developed, recessed or displaced. The bigger the mount, the larger its capabilities.

At first I had some difficulty in distinguishing mounts, but this ability did come in time. It takes years to master palmistry, so don't be discouraged if at first you don't use every aspect in your readings. Mastery comes with time.

The best way to see mounts is to fold over the fingers so that the tips of the fingers are more or less parallel to the palm with the thumb pointing upwards. In this position the mounts hang and become easier to distinguish. Examine them from the side.

Fig. III gives the names of the mounts, and *fig. IV* denotes the general characteristics associated with the mounts. Please memorise this information because we will come back to it time and time again.

Ideally, mounts should have equal influence; each contributing its share, usually in a synchronised way, for the hand is built to be a functioning and integrated unit. However, when the palm is examined you will often observe that one or two mounts dominate. This is reflected in certain personality characteristics. When one or two mounts are dominant, it shows some imbalance. In many cases this imbalance can be utilised effectively. For example, very often Jupiter and Mercury predominate. This configuration favours an active person, and someone engaged in business would find it quite helpful. However, the world is full of, and suffering from, workaholics, which points to an imbalance.

If, for example, the Jupiter mount dominates, the mount area around Jupiter is larger and often easily visible. If there is also a strong Venus, synchronicity can exist. However, if the lunar mount is strong, there is a possibility of incompatibility, because Lunar is passive and Jupiter is active.

Mounts are vibrant, changing as we change, especially in regard to astrological movements and fluctuations in biorhythms. This brings up a very important point, and I will be mentioning it again later: *readings are an 'in the moment' affair*. For example, on some days Venus will be big and strong and on other days it will not be.

When the palm mounts predominate, the hand is considered passive. The focus is more on inner feelings and processes.

When the finger mounts predominate, the hand is an active hand. The focus is primarily on action in the outer world.

I find that developed mounts reflect development and maturity and indicate the person has some capabilities and talents. When the mounts are loose and flabby, usually some laziness is present.

A strong Venus always seems to be good, for that mount channels the main driving force of emotions and mind.

Jupiter and Mercury usually go together and seem to work well when they are dominant.

From just looking at the Saturn mount it is difficult to ascertain if it is dominant. The Saturn finger bending towards the other fingers is a good indication that Saturn is dominating.

A strong Sun mount is always good.

Sometimes a mount is displaced off to one side. This is an indication of trouble or hardship with the characteristics of that mount. Often the Sun mount is off-centre, and this can be an indication of an imbalance in channelling light and creativity.

Characteristics of the mounts

Jupiter

Goals and ambitions, religious ideals. The presentation of one's self to the world. Jupiter is active. When Jupiter is dominant a person is active and outgoing. Jupiter is associated with clarity, brightness and a sense of purpose.

Saturn

Balance, judgements, moral code and sense of belief of ideas. Saturn is active and passive. It gives a foundation to ego functioning.

A dominant Saturn indicates a gloomy person who always sees the dark side, is always critical and allows himself fun only in a limited way, never going over the top. Saturn can be the party pooper. Its colour is blue.

The influence of Saturn is always to regulate, be the watchdog, the moral judge. It is concerned with the mind, with duality, with trying to control and regulate the human condition. Saturn in excess is mostly a drag. It makes a person gloomy and repressed, fixed on selfish ego gratification.

When Saturn is weak, a person does not have a sufficient sense of himself, of what is right and wrong. Saturn provides the moral foundation the ego needs to stand on. Saturn is needed for earth grounding, patience, and a sense of self and morality.

Sun

Light, creativity, warmth in relating. Sun is passive. When the Sun mount is strong a person is in the light, either spiritually or artistically. Brightness and cheerfulness are associated with him.

Mercury

Communication, business, intimate communication in relationships and sexual affairs. A strong Mercury mount is good for business and getting ideas across.

Lunar

Intuition, inner feelings, deep soul connections. A strong Lunar mount shows strong intuition and inner feelings and a person who connects deeply with the collective unconscious.

Venus

Driving life force for emotions, mind and vitality. The bigger the mount the better.

Mars (+)

Power, male driving force, active strength, father love, aggression, accidents, karmic involvement with power, knowing and embodiment of one's own power.

Mars (-)

The passive mount of Mars is involved with courage, passive strength and fortitude. It is the passive side to Mars. It is located directly below the beginning of the heart line, with its south border being the mount of Lunar, and bordered towards the centre by the unconscious central area.

FINGERTIP SHAPES

The ends of the fingers can have different shapes. They range from round to more square to tapering to spatulate. The hand can have all the fingers of one type or there can be a mix.

These different endings affect the character of the mount and/or finger. The reason for this is that energy comes into the hand mostly through the fingertips, which are the main organs for sensitive touch and contain many receptors. The greater the surface area, the greater the number of receptors and the amount of sensitivity. Increased sensitivity is good up to an optimum point and then it becomes a hindrance.

Normal

Nearly everyone has normal fingertips, with slight variations. These fingertips are the round and squarer endings. *See fig. 1.2c, d.* Artistic tapering fingertips are less common, and real spatulate fingertips are rare.

In fact, normal fingertips give the right balance of sensitivity, and mostly we can forget about them during a reading for they are performing their function without flavouring the characteristics of the mount.

Artistic

These are tapering fingertips. The tapering shape increases the ability of the finger to absorb energy, as more receptor surface area is available. People with artistic fingertips are sensitive but not necessarily artistic. They can be of a highly-strung, nervous nature. Often they are refined in some way, always a bit special and needing special care. *See fig.1.2a.*

Spatulate

These fingertips are very rare and persons who have them are sure to have some special talent and/or capability. (I recently gave a reading to a jet fighter pilot who had spatulate fingertips.) The spatulate fingertip is round and becomes wider at the tip of the finger so that it looks like a little pad. This shape gives the best environment for absorbing energy without becoming overloaded. Truly one is lucky to have this fingertip shape. *See fig.1.2b.*

Fingertip shapes can be mixed. Remember, a normal fingertip gives average good absorption while a tapering fingertip increases the sensitivity of the finger. A spatulate fingertip is always good, but it is rare to see just one on a hand. Usually the whole hand has it.

Sensitive fingertips are not always helpful. For example, on Mercury, an increase in sensitivity can be an advantage in communication and intimate relating, but as far as business matters are concerned it is easier when there is not so much sensitivity. This is also true for the Jupiter finger. When you are presenting yourself to the world or are concerned with the fulfilment of goals and ambitions, too much sensitivity can get in the way. When getting on with world affairs and dealing with people it is better to be a bit less sensitive.

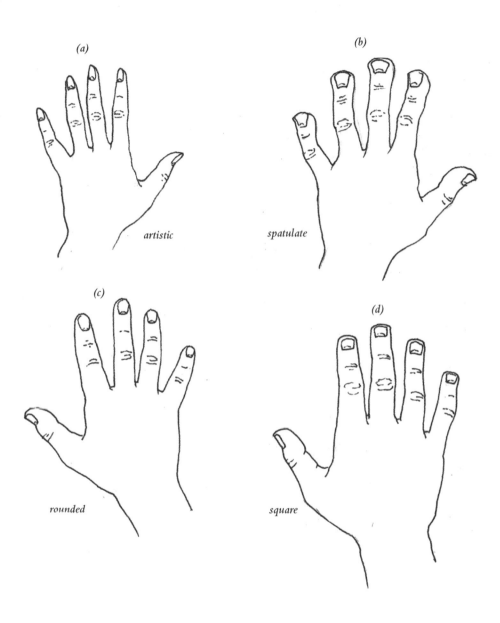

Fig. 1.2 Fingertip Shapes

Nails

It is important to examine the nails. They tell mostly about health and nervous conditions. In a healthy individual, the colour is pink and the nail is smooth and pliable. When nervous conditions are present, the nail is brittle and/or there are striations running through it. When marks and breaks are seen on the head line, make sure you check the nails to see if there is a prevalent nervous condition.

THE SHAPES OF THE FINGERS

A normal, healthy-functioning hand has fingers that are straight and of uniform size, slightly tapering at the tip, and with the three phalanges (vertical divisions) of equal length. These conditions show that proper development has taken place and that the energy of the body flows through the palm and fingers with the least resistance.

When a finger is bent or long or short (in relation to the others), it shows defective development and indicates particular characteristics. For example, a bending of the finger means that cleverness or mind comes to the mount and influences it, usually in a detrimental way.

If there has been unfavourable development in childhood or from past lives (if found in both hands), the fingers will be bent or short or sometimes long. This is especially true of the Jupiter and Mercury fingers.

In a baby's hand, the fingers are undeveloped and are like clay waiting to be moulded. The child's environment greatly determines how the fingers will grow. In a book I once read, the author showed photographs of a child's hand at age five and again at age nine. At age five, the child was an orphan and his Jupiter and Mercury fingers were extremely bent. At that same age he was adopted into a very loving family. At age nine, the photograph showed that his Jupiter and Mercury fingers were straight. This dramatic example shows that nothing in the hand is fixed. Lines and shapes constantly change. This healing also shows the power of love.

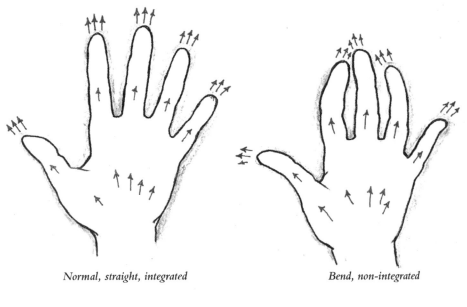

Normal, straight, integrated

Bend, non-integrated

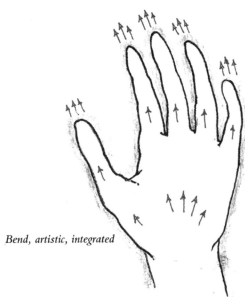

Bend, artistic, integrated

Fig. 1.3 Energy Flow Through the Fingers and Palm

As I have already mentioned, reading a palm really is an *'in the moment' affair. Issues from the past can be resolved and disappear without trace. And they can reappear at any time.*

Bent fingers of Saturn and the Sun are usually present because of karmic reasons involving the development of the 'I am' consciousness rather than childhood development.

The flow of the shape of the palm with the flow of the fingers is very important. The fingers can flow together in an integrated and synchronised way, they can go off in different directions, or they can run into each other. *See fig. 1.3.*

When the flow is integrated, there can be a general curve or arc to the flow, or the energy can flow straight out.

People with fingers going off in different directions or into each other will always have some trouble being straight and clear.

I find that the flow of the energy – how it goes out of the hand from the palm to fingers – is very important. When the energy is bent, crooked and not straight, people are perceived in that way. Very often they are at a complete loss as to why they are always misunderstood. In this regard, there can be much suffering, but it can be diminished with some degree of understanding. With these types, difficulties need to be overcome.

Sometimes only one finger is bent, meaning the person has problems with that particular mount.

People with an arc to flow (bent fingers all flowing smoothly in the same direction) are usually different and creative in a positive way. They do things in a slightly different fashion and people notice them. They are often fashion leaders.

People with straight fingers at least have a full deck to work with. Whether they use it depends on other factors in the hand. They are fortunate in that there is no hindrance to the flow of energy through their fingers. If these people are straight (clear with their intentions) they will be perceived as straight.

Jupiter

The Jupiter finger is considered short when it is shorter than the Sun finger. *See*

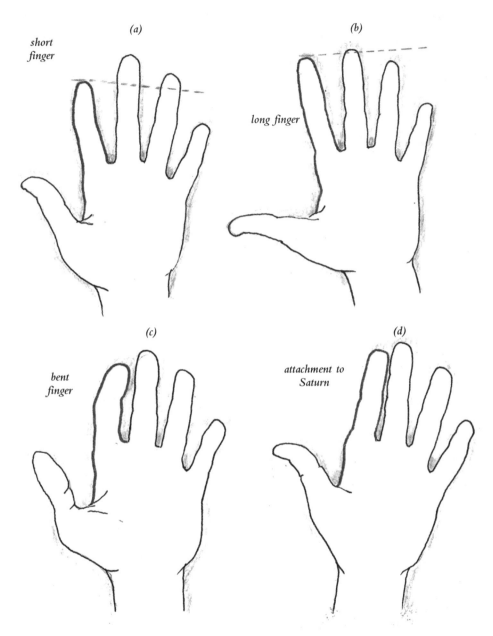

Fig. 1.4 Jupiter

fig.1.4a. They should be of equal length. When Jupiter is short, there are problems with confidence, self-worth and the ability to manifest directly. A very short finger of Jupiter I call the 'Napoleon finger'. This is a rare case, and the holder of this finger has a very strong desire to project his image onto society by being known as a good and important citizen and businessman. As a result, he creates an 'empire' to define himself. The projection of his self-image is more important to him than anything else.

When the finger is only slightly shorter, it means there is a difficulty with fully and directly expressing oneself, one's love or being. A person with this finger needs a medium – painting, for example – in order to express himself fully. Many very good musicians have a short finger of Jupiter.

A long Jupiter finger denotes dominating, bossy qualities, especially if the finger is bent. *See fig.1.4b*. A bent Jupiter means the person is lacking in ability to take responsibility and usually shows some irresponsibility. *See fig.1.4c*.

Mercury

When the finger of Mercury is bent, there is a propensity towards an inability to communicate honestly in intimate relationships and/or to be straightforward in business arrangements. *See fig. 1.5b*. Remember, a bend in a finger brings cleverness or mind to the characteristics of the mount. Very often a knot appears at the joint on this finger. Then it is very clear that the person's mind has a strong influence on how he relates in situations. Spontaneity is difficult. For example, when he finds himself in a situation that makes him angry, instead of just allowing his anger to be present, he first decides if it is appropriate to express it or not. Not expressing anger is not necessarily bad, but processing anger in such a way is fear based, does not reflect a healthy viewpoint and can lead to repression. It is better to cultivate the understanding that anger is a passing emotion, whose rise and fall can be witnessed without expressing it. Although this seems similar, it is a totally different mechanism.

A bent Mercury finger shows some problem in communication on a personal level. This can take the form of judgements, manipulations and

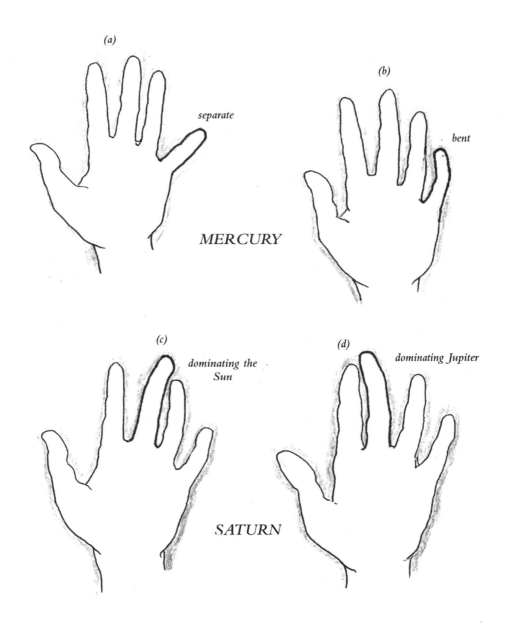

Fig. 1.5 Mercury and Saturn

guarded relations with others. A person with a bent finger of Mercury tends to be dishonest or, let's say, is into bending the truth. The severity of dishonesty depends on other factors. For example, a person with a bent Mercury and strong intuitive head line is more prone to lying and living in a dream world of self-delusion. A broken and fragmented head line indicates a potential lack of integrity, irresponsibility and dishonesty, all of which can lead to lying and a juvenile-type rebellious attitude. If the head line splits the person believes even his own lies. He has a hard time separating illusions from reality. Such a person's stories are never factual, even when he is relating an event that happened minutes ago.

Usually, if the Jupiter or Mercury fingers are bent, they are bent together. In almost all such cases, this is an indication that the person was not loved as a child, and/or was not given the proper nourishment for development, or was in an adverse environment where love and nourishment were difficult to give and receive.

In the case of bent fingers of Mercury, an issue with intimate communication is almost always present. Other factors in the hand must be checked. This you will learn in more detail when I talk about the mount of Mars and the heart line.

Sometimes the Mercury finger is set lower in the hand than the rest of the fingers. *See fig. 1.6.* This indicates that the person will experience hardships in life, whether based on reality or not. A low-set finger of Mercury also indicates trouble in relating to people.

In general, a low-set finger takes away from the quality of the mount.

A good straight finger of Mercury is a sign of honesty and straightness — and is not as common as you might think.

Saturn

The bending of the Saturn finger is a fear-based phenomenon. When making suggestions about behaviour, it is best to point out that behaviours stemming from defective development should not be reinforced but extinguished. This

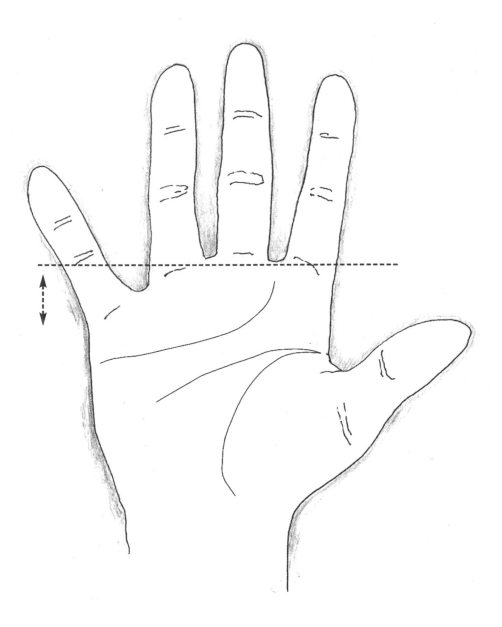

Fig. 1.6 Low-set Mercury Finger

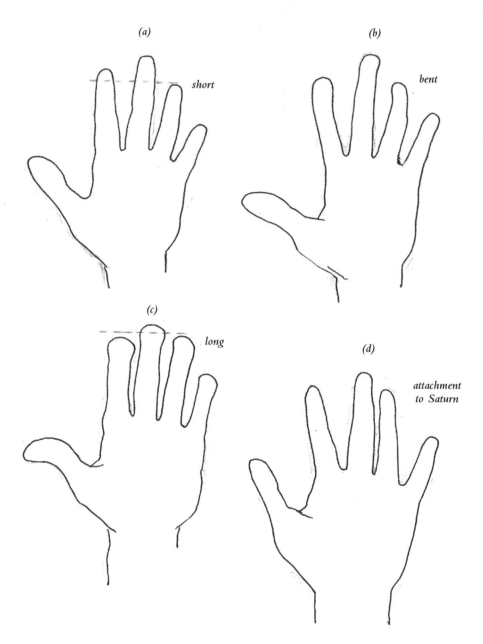

Fig. 1.7 Sun

advice is not so easy to follow, for the tendency is strong and has often been present throughout numerous lives.

When the Saturn finger bends towards the Sun it means that Saturn is trying to cover the Sun, the light. *See fig. 1.5c.* Saturn can be gloomy and not allow creative energy, the spiritual light, to be present and to arise. A person with this hand can be critical of his artistic abilities and can have difficulties showing warmth. This might cause some depression.

When the Saturn finger bends towards Jupiter it states that Saturn is trying to dominate Jupiter. *See fig. 1.5d.* Usually a person with this hand tries to make things happen too forcefully or aggressively. It is difficult for him to just let events and projects happen by themselves. He also wants to make sure everything is right and becomes afraid when it isn't.

Sun

A short Sun finger shows some deficiency: with creative talent, with spiritual light or with the ability to be warm with people. *See fig. 1.7a.* Other factors can compensate for this. A long Sun finger is rare and it can show a special channel for light. *See fig. 1.7c.* Mostly a long finger of Sun is not a hindrance, except when a person becomes obsessed and too identified with being creative.

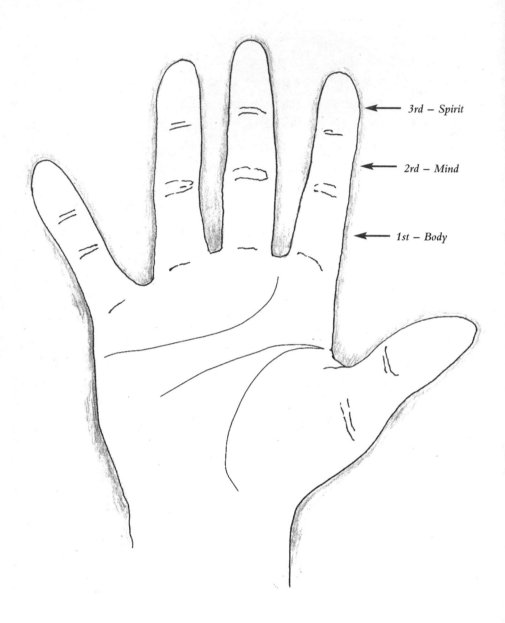

3rd – Spirit

2nd – Mind

1st – Body

Fig. 1.8 Phalanges

THE THREE PHALANGES

Each finger has three divisions, called phalanges. The phalange at the base of the palm represents the body, the middle phalange the mind, and the top phalange the spirit or soul. *See fig. 1.8.* Each phalange reflects the growth of its representative area. A normal finger has phalanges of equal length, showing that the growth of the mind-body-spirit has been good and is in good balance.

If the phalange is long, short or wide, it shows an imbalance.

When a phalange is long, there is more focus on that particular phalange's characteristic. When the phalange is short, there is less emphasis or an inability concerning that phalange's characteristics.

When the first phalange is long there is more focus on the body and fulfilment of sensual pleasures.

On Jupiter, if the first phalange is long, the person's goals are directed towards the body; that is, fulfilment of sensual desires. If coupled with a long first Saturn phalange, the person enjoys the good life and this tends to dominate in his life. Such a person can be ruthless in fulfilling his desires, to the point of betraying friendship.

A long and/or wide first phalange of Saturn shows a liking for the material life.

On Mercury, a long first phalange shows someone who could be good at expressing himself physically, as in giving massage.

In general, if the first phalange is short, there is a basic lack of care concerning the body and the fulfilment of sensual pleasures.

When the second phalange is long, the focus is on action in the physical world. On Mercury, a long second phalange could mean someone is good in business.

If the second phalange is short, action is inhibited or there is a non-caring about it.

When the third phalange is long, spirituality is the main interest. A short third phalange decreases the interest in spirituality.

When the third phalange of Jupiter shows inhibited development – smaller and/or thinner, bent and/or short – the person has problems assuming responsibility.

When the phalanges are of equal or nearly equal length, the person has a normal functioning finger and in a way, as with the shape of the hand, it is just a good vehicle for the other lines and mounts to distribute their currents.

When there are differences in the lengths, the situation becomes more interesting and significant. For example, in my hand the spiritual phalange is the longest while the mind phalange is the shortest. This configuration is an accurate reflection of what I'm like: I am focused mostly on the spiritual realm and my relationship with doing (mind) and the world is quite thin. I hardly have my feet on the ground and the Moon is my only earth sign.

In practice, to measure the phalanges in a reading is time consuming. Mostly the phalanges are of equal length. Usually when the body phalange is long or thick, it is quite noticeable. However, when you notice not-so-obvious differences in length, then there is a payoff in taking the time to measure them.

THE STANDING OF THE FINGERS

When the hand is relaxed, the fingers tend to take a certain position in relation to each other. How the fingers lie with each other gives important information. The optimum way to observe the standing of the fingers is to watch the hand when the subject is naturally relaxed and unaware that you are observing him. If this is not possible, ask the subject to shake his hands for 10 seconds. If this is done a few times, usually a good positioning occurs.

When all the fingers stand a little bit apart, it indicates the person has a well-developed temperament. All his different systems can operate without interference from each other. He can be independent, relate with people or stay alone. Usually such a person is a developed and well-adjusted being.

When the Mercury finger stands some distance apart, it shows a person who not only likes solitude but also needs to be alone for some period of time regularly. *See fig. 1.5a.*

When the Jupiter finger lies separate, it shows independence of action and thinking.

When the Sun finger lies separate it means emotional and creative independence.

When Jupiter and the Sun stand together with Saturn, it means restrictions in the form of moral control from Saturn. The result is a degree of suppression or repression in a way similar to when the Saturn finger bends towards either the Sun or Jupiter finger.

When Saturn and Jupiter are together, it shows that the person's actions, goals and ambitions are influenced by moral judgements, usually in a negative way. *See fig. 1.4d.*

When Saturn and Sun lie together, it means the same in regards to light and creativity. *See fig. 1.7d.* Saturn is inhibiting creativity and spiritual light from flowing in a natural and spontaneous way. The attachment to Saturn is fear based. The flow of each mount is restricted. Caution is present, as is a person's desire to hide and not show himself.

Clinging to Saturn indicates dependency and the inability to act freely.

THE THUMB

The thumb is an extremely important part of the hand. Without it we would be in trouble. They say that the development of the thumb is what separates us from animals. It enables us to make dexterous manipulations that thumbless animals cannot manage. No wonder the thumb is associated with life-force energy, logic and willpower.

The thumb is active.

The thumb has three parts: the mount of Venus and the second and third phalanges.

The mount of Venus holds the life-force energy, which includes love energy, sexual energy and vital energy. This force powers the second phalange of logic and the third phalange of willpower.

The length of the second and third phalanges should be in the ratio of three to two respectively. This ratio creates a good balance between logic and willpower. When the length of the second phalange exceeds this ratio (see *fig. 1.9a*), the person is more of a dreamer and the manifestation of ideas is slower than the thought process that created them. This very often leads to frustration, because though the person can very quickly see how to do something in his mind, manifesting it takes much longer. I have found that in most hands the second phalange of logic is longer than the third phalange of willpower.

When the third phalange is greater, the stronger willpower makes the person more impulsive, acting without sufficient thought to what he is doing. *See fig. 1.9b.*

Other factors, such as the strength of Jupiter and the head line, must always be checked. These can modify the above tendencies significantly.

From my observation of many hands it is my conclusion that the length of the thumb is extremely important and that even a quick glance can reveal much about the person's capabilities. The longer the thumb the better. *See fig. 1.10c.* This is especially true when the thumb is straight and not waisted. I associate integrity with a longer thumb. The person has more capability for doing and acting, and is therefore more reliable. A longer thumb means the person can act and get both ideas and life together. Persons with long thumbs are more likely to be expressive in their communications. Leaders usually have long thumbs.

With a short thumb, there are usually difficulties around manifesting in the physical world. *See fig. 1.10d.* People with short thumbs are usually not doers, or they are doers but more effort is needed to complete projects. Short-thumb people are usually more passive and can develop in the inner worlds without problems.

The thumb can be set high or low in the hand. *See fig. 1.10a, b.* A low-set thumb generally shows a person who is capable of giving and able to encompass more of life. This person possesses compassion. A low-set thumb is always a good indication that the person has giving qualities.

When the thumb and Jupiter fingers are stretched apart the size of the angle shows how much a person is capable of giving. *See fig. 1.11a.* The larger the angle, the more giving a person is, basically because physically he is able to handle more. If there is resistance to this stretch, he has some degree of stubbornness or resistance to giving is present.

Very often the tip of the thumb has a natural backwards tilt. This shows that the person has some degree of natural openness and is ready to be spontaneous.

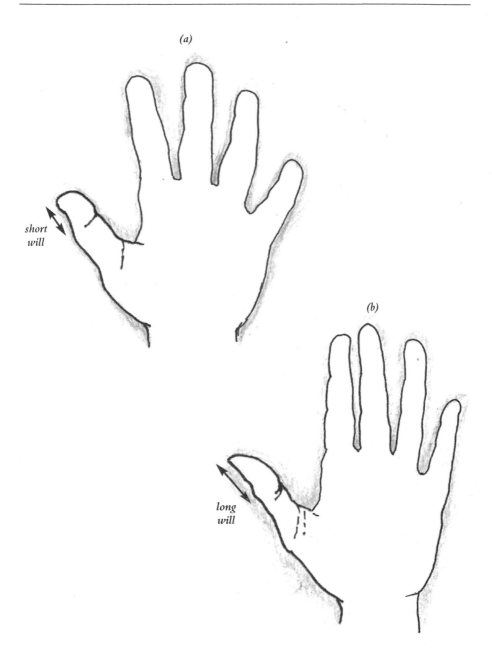

Fig. 1.9 Thumbs I

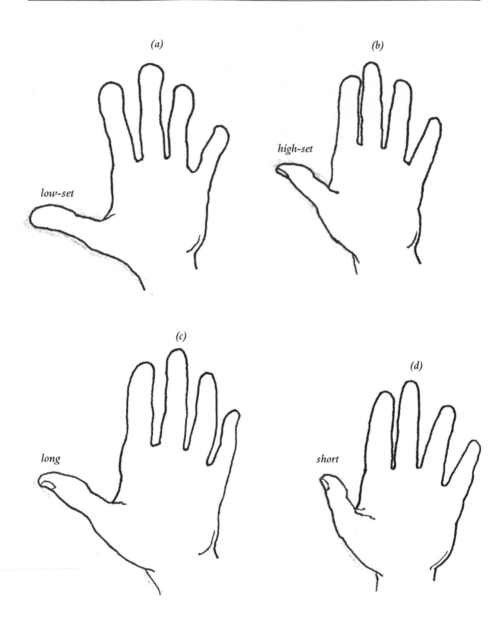

Fig. 1.10 Thumbs II

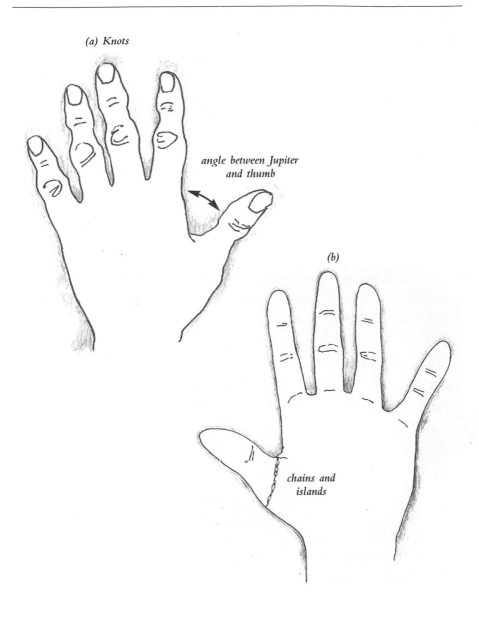

(a) Knots

angle between Jupiter and thumb

(b)

chains and islands

Fig. 1.11 Knots, Line Between Thumb and Venus

If there is a knot or thickening between the phalanges, it means some problems with anger, and frustration can be present. The more waisted the thumb, the greater the possibility of sudden outbursts of anger, which can be violent depending on other factors in the hand. The 'murderer's thumb' is a club thumb, where the third phalange is much bigger and wider than the second.

A good thumb is one that is smooth and straight and of good length. It means no resistance to action.

There is a line that separates the mount of Venus from the thumb. *See fig. 1.11b.* If this line is chained or broken, it means the person will have hardships in life.

When the thumb is bent backwards, it can bend easily or it can be stiff. If it bends easily, it shows flexibility in action; a person is able to change directions easily. A stiff thumb shows that the person has some difficulty moving in spontaneous ways, being in the moment and able to change directions easily. The person can be quite liberal or even radical in design, but once a decision has been taken there is difficulty in switching to another direction.

How a person positions the thumb can tell much. If a person is open, the thumb will be out and available. If a person is closed or scared, the thumb will be either pressed against Jupiter or hidden in the palm. If the person is angry, he will exhibit a closed fist with the thumb inside.

KNOTS

At the joints of each finger there can be a solid-feeling bulge, and this is called a knot. *See fig. 1.11a.* Knots mean 'the mind'. The energy of that mount must first be filtered through the mind before it can proceed into its channel. A person with knotty fingers is usually slow to act, highly intellectual and can often have problems relating to himself and others.

When a knot is observed on a finger, immediately add mind, intellect and slowness. Mind can mean cleverness, manipulation and judgements. For example, on Mercury, the holder is not spontaneous in relationships, although once he does get moving he is okay. Some patience is needed with a knotted Mercury finger.

A knot on the Sun finger influences creativity by making it slow moving. The person thinks out the whole project beforehand. This can be good but can interfere with spontaneous creative impulses.

On the Saturn finger knots are definitely not good. They make the person even more repressed.

On Jupiter, knots make the person very controlled in how he presents himself to the world.

On the thumb a knot is not a good sign. There is potential for a bottleneck of energy leading to frustration and outbursts of energy, usually in the form of anger, to relieve the bottleneck.

In general, knots on the first joint make the holder more attached to body and desires because of a resistance of flow into higher channels. This inertia can keep him from flying higher into deeper layers of being and also gives the holder a predisposition to physical diseases. People with knotty fingers often fall ill easily.

FINGERPRINTS

Each person has a unique individual fingerprint, although there are only four basic fingerprint patterns. *See fig. 1.12*. Each pattern tells a story, because there seems to be a very good correlation between fingerprint pattern and certain personality characteristics. There is also an excellent correlation between the pattern and the level of development of the corresponding mount's characteristics.

Fingerprints tell a big story, and it is not possible for me to give a reading without knowing the subject's fingerprint patterns.

The basic fingerprint types are:
- Arch
- Loop
- Composite
- Whorl

A hand can have all the fingerprints of the same type or there can be a mixture. When there are more than six of one fingerprint type, then that type is the predominant fingerprint. The arch and loop patterns are the most common.

Arch

The arch pattern is the simplest form, and the arch fingerprint can vary greatly from a hardly rising simple arch to a very complex steeply rising arch.

When the arch is simple and hardly rising, it shows that development on that mount is slight, and very often issues arise because of the need for further development. For example, on Jupiter, a simple arch can mean a lack of talent for presenting oneself or an inability to take responsibility.

People with arch patterns tend to be closed and not immediately open to change. This is due mostly to a lack of development rather than an unwillingness to be open.

A more complex arch that rises shows that some development of the mount has occurred but this development is still of a simple nature. If the arch rises straight up, it shows a bit of stiffness and a resistance to spontaneity regarding the characteristics of that mount.

Loop

The loop contains two elements: a slight arch and a looping pattern above it, which can swing either left or right. The addition of the loop brings more complexity than the arch pattern alone and is a reflection of increased development. The loop is most common and normally denotes average intelligence and development. The loop itself indicates some openness and spontaneity and a willingness to flow.

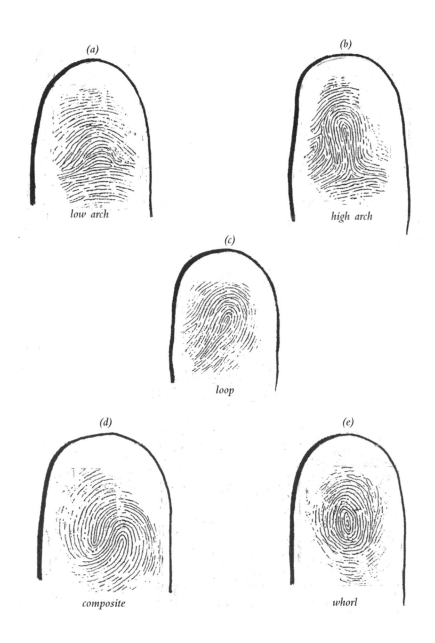

Fig. 1.12 Fingerprint Patterns

Composite

This print originates from the joining of two pattern flows that form a composite print.

If the person is a composite type or has a composite print on a finger and especially the thumb, always look for duality of characteristics and/or compartmentalisation of characteristics and perceptions. The person can be a certain way in one area and completely opposite in another. This is especially true if the composite print is on the thumb or Jupiter. Such a person can also compartmentalise subjects and areas. One woman I know, when she goes to work in Germany, goes there only to work and nothing else. 'Germany is where I work,' she says. 'Playing happens somewhere else.'

Another woman who has a composite thumb is very sweet and loving when she is being just a friend, but as soon as money and survival are involved, she becomes ruthless, ready to kill, and is very hard and tough.

In this way, with composite types, you will see some kind of split, although not always negative and not always not integrated.

Whorl

Whorl types are unique and the most individualistic. The whorl pattern is the only type where a very particular personality is present (to the degree of being a stereotype). They love their independence and must live in their own peculiar way, no matter how much they have to sacrifice to do so. These types are usually eccentric, live in isolated areas and often are involved with nature and animals. They would rather live in an isolated forest, having their own small kingdom, than in a city or village where there are more material riches and friendships.

A whorl shows that some exceptional degree of development has occurred in that mount, whether the characteristic is dormant or utilised in this life.

To have just one or two whorls is very auspicious.

A whorl on the Sun finger, especially if only on the two Sun fingers, shows that the person truly has luck and can count on it. Luck will always enter into his life, one way or another. In fact, even if all other aspects of the hand are unfavourable, he will excel in life, receiving wealth, prestige, insight and intelligence.

A whorl on a finger indicates advanced development of the characteristics of that mount. If it is on Jupiter, the person has a developed ability to present himself. Either through past-life work or through grace, achievement of a high order is present. This evolvement might be dormant and not even used. There can be several reasons for this. One reason may be that other areas need to be developed, and if that particular advancement were present, it would inhibit the development of these other areas. Another reason is that a block could have developed. In this case, the person can access the ability when he really needs it – that is, if he can find the key to open the door.

A whorl on Mercury means good communication, good business sense and refinement in the area of intimate relationships. Flow is easy and quick.

On Saturn, a whorl shows that how a person uses forces and creates balance is highly developed and a deep sense of groundedness is present.

A whorl on the thumb shows development in logic and willpower. The movement of life force will have no resistance. Goals and ideas will manifest seemingly without lifting a finger.

A predominance of whorls (more than six) doesn't necessarily mean that the mounts have made developmental achievements; rather, it is an indication of the whorl-type personality. Whether achievements are present or not is determined in the reading. When there is a predominance of whorls, the story becomes more complicated and the achievements somehow take a back seat. Very often an excess of mental and creative development creates a mind-body-soul energy field that is too intricate, too complicated to function effectively. The whorl-type person seeks solitude because he is overdeveloped and can't handle the normal stress of being in society. This is especially true when there are many lines in the hands that go in all different directions. Always I advise such an individual not to go on creating and developing, but to simplify. We are so conditioned to create, create and create that it can get in the way. In my opinion, such a type needs to go beyond creating and discover what or who is doing the creating. In this instance creating is an obstacle to discovering his own true self.

Perhaps a whorl type is so developed that he cannot simply be part of the normal world but must live apart from it. He is so developed and complicated that he appears to be eccentric. Usually this type is suffering in some way because of his uniqueness and individuality.

Developing the mind-body personality is beneficial up to a point. Afterwards it becomes a hindrance to further growth. Creation and the development of the mind-body personality are not the end point of evolution but a step on the way. We tend to get lost by creating more and more, by becoming too complex and complicated. Further growth requires looking deep within ourselves to find the source of our own self. And this source lies beyond creation and the mind and personality.

PALMPRINTS

There can be on the palm characteristic skin patterns similar to fingerprints. *See fig. 1.13.*

A whorl near the end of the head line usually means the person has a good memory, very often a photographic memory, and/or can remember past events quite well.

When this whorl is located further down in the Moon area, it indicates a person who has charisma and a magnetic personality. Papaji, a great Indian spiritual master of recent times, had an incredibly big whorl on the lunar side, covering a large portion of his palm. His magnetism and influence on people were very strong.

Under the Sun finger, a whorl means a sense of humour. If the whorl is displaced to the side, then the opposite, seriousness, is implicated.

A skin pattern between the Saturn and Jupiter fingers means serious intent and is often present on the palms of healers.

In my practice, I've found only the above-mentioned patterns. In other books you can find more patterns, and I suggest you study them. Always remember, the hands that I see are those of a limited number of people mostly from the same subculture. In the subgroups that you will be looking at, you may find completely different patterns and arrangements.

I find variations even within a subgroup, and I have noticed at particular

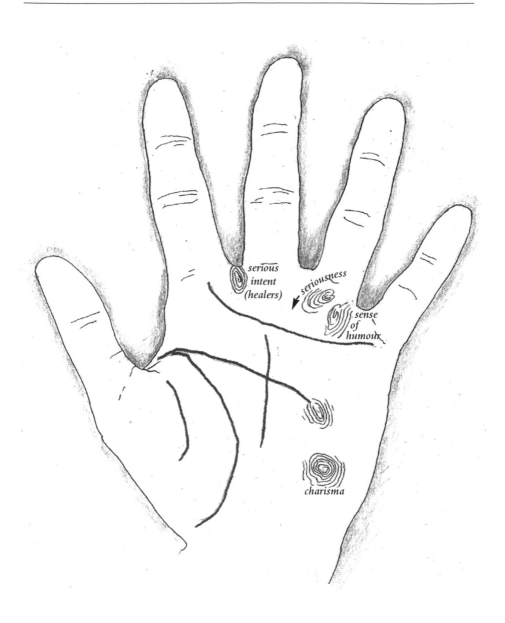

Fig. 1.13 Palmprint Patterns

periods certain patterns seem to repeat. For example, at the moment I am visiting a spiritual community in the Himalayas and almost all the hands I've looked at have some similar characteristics. I found in almost all of the hands (mostly women's) some indication of past-life violence and aggression. There are strong, intense markings on the positive mount of Mars on the passive hand, and on the active hand as well, although here there are fewer markings.

Chapter 2

THE LINES:
AN INTRODUCTION

The lines on the palm have fascinated us since we have had the intelligence to perceive them and make associations and conclusions about them. In the West, the first written treatise on hands was compiled by Aristotle, and it is quite accurate. In India, palmistry is as ancient a science as astrology, going back thousands upon thousands of years to the time of the *Vedas* (ancient scriptures) and *rishis* (holy persons).

The lines on the palm are alive, vibrant and constantly changing. They do not exist only because of the way the hand folds. The lines are deeply connected to the central nervous system and change as we change. When the nerves in the arm that lead to the hand are cut, the lines on the palm will disappear. Therefore, the lines are a reflection of our vibrant nature and can be used to indicate mental, emotional and spiritual states.

How the form of the lines became associated with the form of our mental-emotional-spiritual personalities is a mystery, as is everything else. What is important is that the association exists. Over the vast expanse of time, it has been found that when a certain line is present, a certain trait, talent or tendency, or a certain way of perceiving the world, is also present. This association is similar to the way in which, in astrology, the planets and their movements are associated with certain types of influences upon us.

There is no hocus-pocus involved in the association of lines and human characteristics. The connections are quite scientific. Hocus-pocus enters when a interpretation is made from the scientific observations. A good interpretation relies greatly on intuition, and intuition is as scientific as logic. A good reading involves a skilful use of both intuition and logic.

Palmistry is a tool to help us see ourselves and understand the mechanics of our mind-body mechanism. It is as valid as any branch of psychology or astrology. You might be surprised how much of our mind-body mechanism is purely mechanical and robot like.

Now let us look at the blueprint of our mind-body-spirit mechanism. The lines of the palm can be divided into primary and secondary lines.

Primary lines – life lines, head lines and heart lines – are always present in the palm, except in very rare cases. Secondary lines – Saturn, Sun, Mars, liver, Girdle of Venus – are not always present in the palm but are as important as the primary lines.

There are a few general points to know about lines, which apply to all of them.

First, begin to see the lines as energy channels or canals. The lines are an indication of how the energy of the lines travels and flows. An ideal line is one that is strong and continuous, showing no breaks, chains or marks Breaks, islands, chains or marks are a sign of weakness, indicating some resistance to flow. There is an exception to this rule. If a line breaks but a new line starts before the break, 'a change in direction' is the indicated meaning rather than 'weakness'.

A line that is wide, deep and showing a strong red colour indicates a strong passionate energy. This is true of Caucasian, Western people, but recently I've discovered that in Indian palms this is not the case. Nearly all Indians have thick red lines, but this does not necessarily indicate passion.

Lines can be pale or more diffuse. Paleness means less energy, at least on the surface. I massage the palm to see if the lines become redder. If they do, it means the subject's energy is hidden but can be brought out when activated. When massaging the palm does not make the lines redder, it can be a sign that there is a weak hold on life, less attachment to life, and/or only a limited amount of energy available to the subject.

Chapter 3

PRIMARY LINES

LIFE LINE
'River of Life'

The life line starts somewhere between the top of the base of the thumb and the base of Jupiter, and runs usually in a semi-circular curve around the mount of Venus, ending at the bottom of the palm right before the rasceltes or bracelets. The life line shows the strength of the life force and the general course of life from birth to death. This includes events of life, influxes and outflows of energy, available energy at a given period in the life, weakness, illnesses, peak experiences and, of course, death.

The life line is male and active.

Beginnings

The life line should start just on the front side of the palm. If it starts behind the palm then some excess is present, which if also seen in other lines can mean mental imbalance. People with this excess are usually extreme and subject to mental collapses. This is also true if the life line begins with a downward slope.

The beginning of the life line shows how the soul connects to or enters the

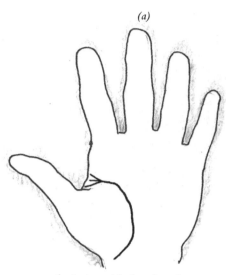

(a)

beginning with three branches

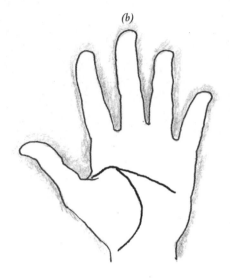

(b)

beginning with a downward slope

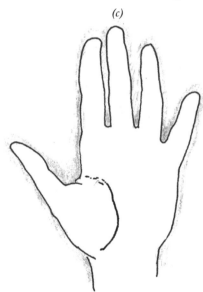

(c)

beginning weakly

Fig. 3.1   Life Lines

body. If the connection has been good, the line starts full, straight and continuous. If the line is broken in some way or is not straight and continuous, there has not been a good connection. When there has not been a good connection with the body, the person is usually rather spaced out and not grounded in the body. His focus is geared more to the inner world rather than the physical world. Most likely he will not become a professional athlete.

Another possible meaning for the above conditions is childbirth difficulties and/or illness at birth. This can be verified by checking the beginning of the heart line, which gives information about childbirth. Correlating information from different areas is very important for the palmist; it can make the difference in a reading when there is a firm confirmation. In general, a person whose life line does not start properly has difficulty accepting his role in life and manifesting in the world. If he is of a spiritual persuasion, this difficulty can be used to his advantage, for the troubles of life can help to turn his focus inwards.

Sometimes two or more lines come together to form the life line. *See fig. 3.1a.* This means that several life forces (rays of creation) are coming together to create a particular incarnation. It indicates a special incarnation but not necessarily an easy one.

The life line is male or yang, for it shows what is present in the positive, materialistic sense of how the life flows in the material world.

If the beginning of the life line has a downward slope, it is an indication of a malady, usually something from a past life of a serious nature. It is not an auspicious sign. *See fig. 3.1b.*

Course of Life Showing Splits, Breaks, Marks and Variations

The life line and head line very often start together, run together and then split, with the life line arching downwards while the head line goes out into the frontier of the palm. Generally the area where the lines run together represents early childhood until early adulthood when a person leaves the family to be on his own. If his environment, sense of security and emotional and psychological development were good, this joined line will be straight and continuous. Indications of difficulty in early childhood include chains, a thin or weak line, marks on the lines and slashes running across the life line (hatchworks). This difficulty can manifest as inhibited development, major illness, an accident or any detrimental event – by itself or in combination, depending upon the severity and number of markings.

Often you will see (or just have a sense of) an unstable line, which is a reflection of the environment the child grew up in. With an unstable line, trust of the world can be lacking. *See fig. 3.1c.* Correlate this with the shape of Jupiter and Mercury fingers. If they are undeveloped or bent then it is almost certain that the childhood was unstable.

Indication of a difficult childhood by the early part of the life line is always correct, no matter how much the subject insists it was normal. At some point during the reading the subject will always reveal the truth about his childhood. Very often people don't even realise how unstable their childhoods were.

Slashes crossing the early part of the life line indicate major accidents, major illnesses, and possible physical or psychological abuse from the father, especially if the slashes originate from the mount of Mars.

The life line shows the general course of the life. The line can become thicker or thinner in places; this shows fluctuations in life force or periods of abundance and scarcity. An island means a period of weakness; the life force is split so the person is more vulnerable to influences and sensitive to changes. Weakness is indicated when you see an island on any line. *See fig. 3.2d.*

It is important to begin to understand that the lines are always a reflection of *now*. If there is an island in the middle of the life line, it can mean a period of weakness in midlife, and/or it can mean that the life-force energy will encounter a period of weakness whenever it flows. And this weakness will have to be compensated for by additional effort or perseverance. Extra energy will be needed to complete actions in life. Because the lines are constantly changing, when this weakness is gone, the island will disappear.

Small lines starting above the life line and ending exactly on the life line are an indication of an influx of divine energy. *See fig. 3.2b.* During this time, the person will receive an additional influx in the form of a spiritual experience, peak experience and/or increase in wealth. The most common influx is the spiritual experience. In a way, it can be thought of as a cosmic bonus, or what is in India called 'a boon'.

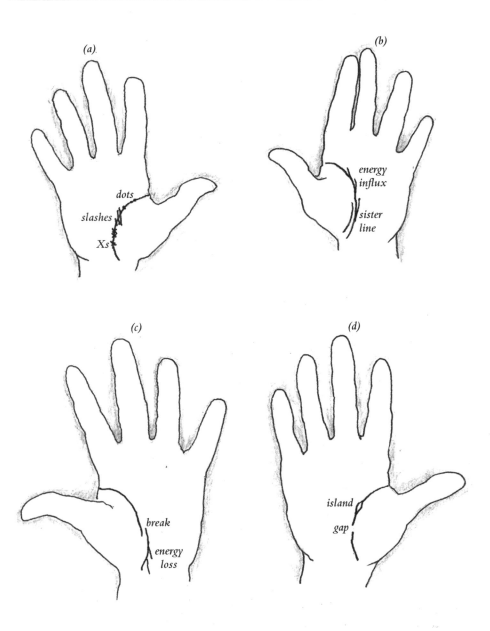

Fig. 3.2 Life Line Markings

Small downward lines starting precisely on the life line mean a loss of energy, usually illness. *See fig. 3.2c.*

If the life line breaks or stops and another line starts before the break, it means that the person will have a radical change in life direction. He may, for example, change from leading a secular life to a spiritual one, or vice versa. *See fig. 3.2c.*

A distinct gap in the life line means that for that period of time the person has no hold on the life force. *See fig. 3.2d.* Anything can happen. Death or spiritual enlightenment is very possible at that time. If the head line is strong, most likely the person won't die. It is a very opportune time for the person to experience reality beyond the confines of body, mind, personality and destiny.

If the life line remains without breaks and marks, the course of the life will be smooth. If there are breaks and marks, there will be struggle and hardships. *See fig. 3.2a, c.*

Endings

The ending of the life line is important. When downward lines at the end of the life line are present, the person will lose energy, usually through illness. *See fig. 3.3a.* If the life line is weak after the downward slash, the person should plan for his old age because he will not have full energy to take care of himself. If the line remains strong, he will recover and be active again. If the life line has many branches at the end or is tasselled, it means the person's life will disintegrate. *See fig. 3.3b.* And usually he will battle with this issue of disintegration throughout his life. He will start projects, continue them for a while and then collapse. You can only recommend that such a person looks after himself and does not resort to dissipating activities such as taking drugs, for example. But this advice is difficult to follow since the tendency is karmic and must be played out.

The life line can end in the following ways:

- Strong and straight. This shows that the person will be active until the end.
- With many tassels. The life force will disintegrate and there may be hardships at the end. Tassels can be an indication of dementia and Alzheimer's disease.

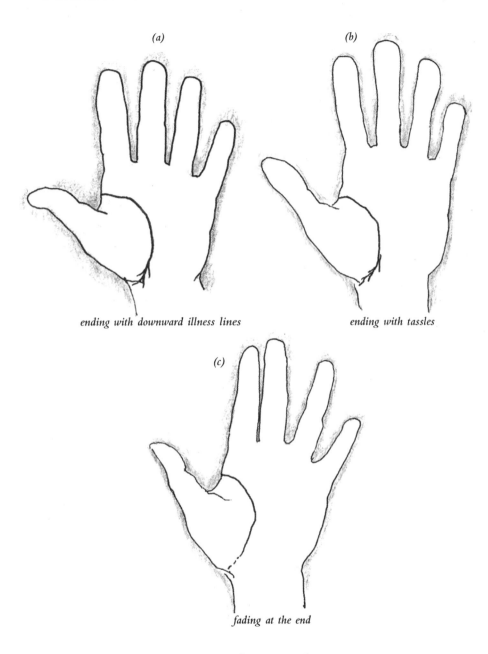

(a)

(b)

ending with downward illness lines

ending with tassles

(c)

fading at the end

Fig. 3.3 Life Line Endings

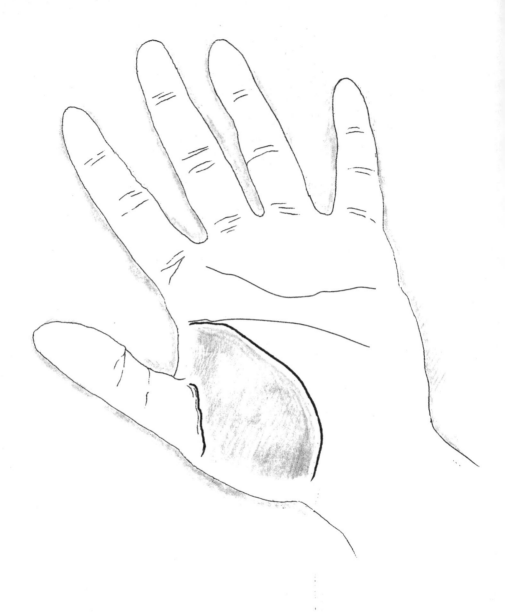

Fig. 3.4 Area of the Life Line

- Thin and fading. *See fig. 3.3c.* This shows a general disappearance back into the void. Usually it is gentle and benign. The last years are not very active, but not necessarily senile.
- Strong with downward illness lines. This means illness in later years. The person will not be active and must be taken care of.

The area the arc of the life line covers shows the scope of the person's consciousness. *See fig. 3.4.* The broader the arc, the broader his scope, horizon and outlook. Narrow life line areas usually mean narrow-minded people, although a person could simply be living a quiet life with no need for a broad outlook. Sometimes the area of the life line is broader in the active hand. This increase in area can be the result of the formation of a new life line. The greater area indicates an increase in the scope of consciousness of the person in this life, and is a very important aspect when present.

If the end of the life line goes into or towards the Moon area, it means the person will live and most probably die in a foreign country. How a person dies, and from what diseases, is determined by the strength and weakness of the head and heart line.

Often I see the end of the life line radically changing, going through a metamorphosis, with lines splitting and other lines merging to form a new ending. Sometimes a Saturn line merges with the life line to form a new ending. This happens more often than not, and shows that in many instances the end of the life is not fixed but is determined by something else unknown. In such cases, I tell the subject that his destiny is not fixed; his path in life can proceed in many different directions. At some point, choices will be made that determine the direction, though the choices will not necessarily be conscious ones on his part.

The subject of destiny is always a *question*. The changing ending of the life line can be evidence that destiny is not always fixed. However, it could be someone's destiny to not have a fixed destiny. In cases where the life line is changing, people often ask me about their destiny and in which direction they should move.

Challenge and Influence Lines

Challenge and influence lines are an integral part of the life line and can't really be separated from it. Lines, usually originating from the mount of Mars, which cross the life line are called life challenge lines. *See fig. 3.5.* These lines mean that life presents challenges that cannot be avoided. If a person tries to avoid them, his level of suffering will increase until he begins to meet the challenge. To determine at what time in the life these challenges will appear is difficult, because these lines commonly appear and disappear. A challenge line means *now* and can cover a period of one to two years in the past or future. A challenge line also can mean that a challenge will be encountered at the particular age where it crosses the life line. The intuitive ability of the palmist decides which situation is prevalent. I approach challenge lines as mostly being *now*, because they disappear once the challenge is over. If a challenge line represented only challenges at a particular age, the line would not disappear.

When challenge lines cross throughout the life line, a person will never be at rest. A person without challenge lines can also be suffering with no rest but for different reasons.

Challenge lines indicate life lessons coming from seemingly external events.

When there are many, many lines crossing the life line, especially by the mount of Mars, it means psychic interference. The person usually feels exhausted and tired all the time. On a subconscious level, much energy is being used to counteract this psychic noise. Psychic interference can be compared to static on a radio programme. You can listen for a while, but it is annoying and you feel drained by it. This interference usually occurs as some sort of karmic debt, but it can be cleared up very successfully by meditation, *pujas* (prayer rituals) or some sort of exorcism.

When a line crosses the life line and intersects with the head line, it is a line of influence. *See fig. 3.5.* It means someone or something is having a profound effect upon the person. If it also crosses the heart line, it is an ever greater influence, getting into the person's heart and soul. If this line contacts the Saturn

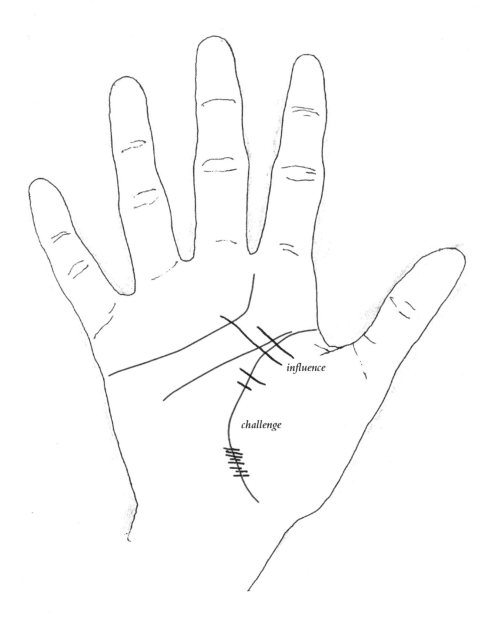

influence

challenge

Fig. 3.5 Challenge and Influence Lines

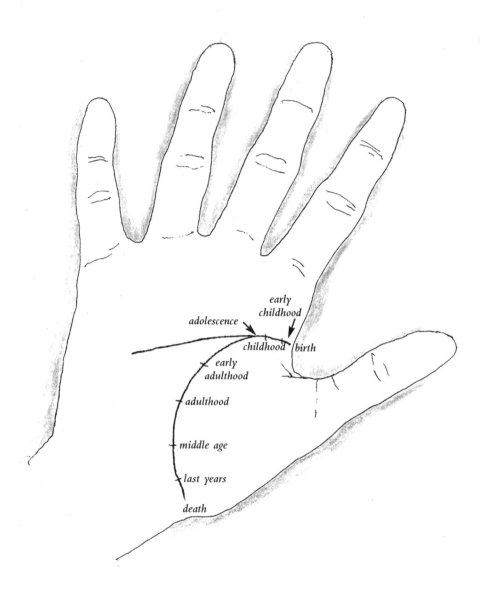

Fig. 3.6 Timings of the Life Line

line, someone or something is influencing the wealth of the person. Whether the influence is positive or negative needs to be determined. If the line goes into an island or a break of some sort, it is probably a negative influence.

What is the special significance of influence lines, because after all aren't events and people constantly influencing us? Influence lines are significant because they show that a strong karmic influence is operating and having a major impact on the course and direction life takes. When an influence line runs into the heart line, for example, it shows that the major focus for the time it appears on the palm is the further development of the heart. At this time it is good for the person to focus on the affairs of the heart and spiritual matters.

The length of the life line alone does not necessarily show how long a person will live. The other lines also play a major role. For example, short head lines on both hands, together with short or faint life lines, usually mean a short life. *A person can live without a life line but not without a head line.* As I have not examined the hands of recently dead people, I can't say this is my direct observation. However, on an intuitive level this feels correct. I have seen instances of a short life line or no life line in people who have gone on to live very long lives.

Sometimes there is a small sister line running along the life line for some distance. This means added strength for the duration of the sister line.

Timings

The life line can be divided into several distinct areas – birth, early childhood, childhood, adolescence, early adulthood, adulthood, middle age, last years and end of life. *See fig. 3.6.*

I keep timings as general as I can – ten-year increments usually. However, this is my way. Another reader can use more precise timings, if that is what he desires.

The best system I've discovered is based on two landmarks. *See fig. 3.7.* The first is determined by drawing a straight line from the middle of the gap between the Jupiter and Saturn fingers to the life line. Where the line intersects the life line can be considered age 21.

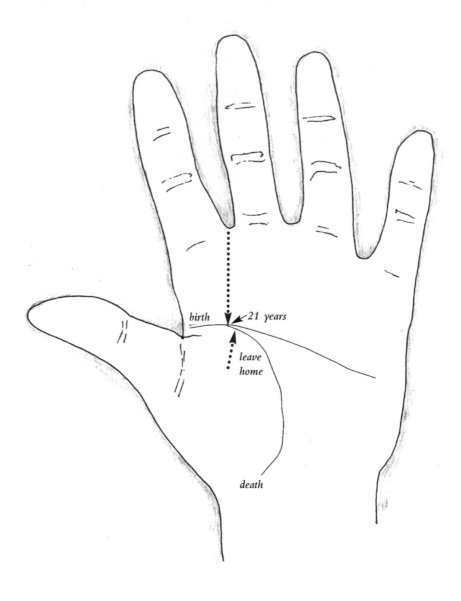

Fig. 3.7 Timings

The second landmark only applies when the life line and head line are joined together. As this is the case with the majority of hands, mostly it can be used. Ask the subject at which age he left his family to live on his own. Generally, where the two lines split is that age. Compare the landmarks and if they are close, use them. If not, take an average and make a general estimate. Also, just guess if someone asks; your guess will usually be right! You can divide the life line into childhood, early adulthood, adulthood, middle age and later years based on the period indicated by the landmark you have determined.

You must remember that lines are not dead or static but vibrant and changing. The lines are always a reflection of now. So what does time in an exact way mean in lines? I've recently watched the beginning of my life line restructure itself in such a dramatic way that I would now give myself a reading very different from the one I gave five years ago. The significance of this observation has led me to wonder about and question everything I know about palmistry.

Basically, I've come to realise that the lines are a reflection of now, this moment. Past, present, future and the eternal are in reality one, each modifying the other in ways we cannot understand. Can the future modify the past? From my observation of lines, I can accept the possibility of this notion.

HEAD LINE
'How We See the World'

The head line starts somewhere near the beginning of the life line and runs out across the palm, ending somewhere near, on the edge of, or in the Lunar mount itself. If the head line reaches Saturn, it is considered of normal length. It is very rare for the head line not to reach Saturn.

The head line represents the energy channel of the mental body. The head line has two basic categories, and in this respect is different from the life line which has only one. The heart line also has two basic categories.

Category 1 is determined at the beginning of the line, when the head line starts either *with* the life line or *separate* from it.

Category 2 is determined by how the head line runs across the frontier of the palm after it leaves the life line. The head line can run straight across the palm or it can dip into the lunar area.

Between the two categories there is much variation and each variation has a specific meaning.

Category 1

Head line and life line joined together (*fig. 3.8a*)

When the head line begins with the life line, it means that most if not all perceptions pass through the mind. The majority of people have this confluence and it is more prevalent in men. This joining of lines means there is attachment and desire to stay close to the life force, in the form of family and society. There is a dependency upon family, society and morality. The longer the lines run together, the greater the attachment.

When the head and life line run together for a long distance, it indicates resistance to growing up. This resistance can be traced back to trauma at birth and even before, to the point of reincarnating. People with long running lines don't want to grow up, they want to remain children and as a result are immature for a long time. They did not even want to be born and take on another life. Such persons are very cautious and don't want to take risks. The key word for this category of head line is 'caution'. 'Weigh the facts and make a decision.' The mind is filtering the perceptions, wanting to figure things out before acting. Such caution is fear based. And the longer the lines run together, the greater the reluctance to grow up.

An example of such a type is a medical doctor I know, a man in his late 40s who is quite intelligent and perceptive. However, whenever I walked into his room, it was like being in the room of an 8-year-old boy. It was always a complete mess and cluttered with adult toys. When I looked at his hand I understood why – he had the longest running-together life and head line I'd ever seen. Almost halfway down his life line. This man has had problems growing up and taking real responsibility. He has got into trouble with his medical licence and generally behaves just like a little boy, especially with women.

The point where the head and life line split is usually the time when a person becomes independent *on a psychological level* and leaves the family home. A

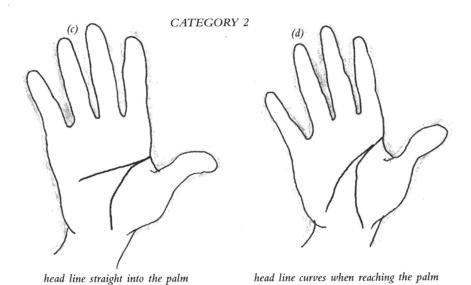

CATEGORY 1

(a)

(b)

head line and life line joined together

head line separate from life line

CATEGORY 2

(c)

(d)

head line straight into the palm

head line curves when reaching the palm

Fig. 3.8 Head Line Categories

person could live separately from the family and still be totally dependent upon it. I discuss the situation with the subject to determine if this is the case.

The joining of the head and life line is a very good indication that the personality of the subject is fear based. And since in the majority of hands the head and life line are joined, the majority of people are fear based. In the enneagram (an ancient Sufi teaching describing nine different personality types and their interrelationships) this corresponds to types 5, 6 and 7.

Head line separate from life line (fig. 3.8b)

When the head line is separate from the life line it means the person is independent, has the ability to organise and has a natural affinity for being alone, because he can feel complete when alone. There is less interference from the mind, so action can be more direct and more to the point. This results in spontaneity and the ability to perceive reality directly without using the mind.

This type of head line is more prevalent in women. The separation of the life line shows that the person has a certain amount of freedom from society, family and morality. He can be independent from the influence of parents, which gives more freedom of action. This is not to say that a person with the life and head line joined cannot act and do in the world. Many can and do so quite easily. However, the basic gestalt when the lines are separate is different because the mind is not filtering the life-force energy.

An individual with separate head and life lines has the ability to think and act clearly, but often a person with these lines is surprised to learn he has this ability. In this case other factors are strongly influencing the trait. The thumb, the strength of the heart line, and Jupiter also play a major role. Blocks can be present and the quality of the line will be hidden; however, there is always a possibility of accessing it, so it is important to discuss this with the individual.

The distance between head line and life line is important. The bigger the distance, the weaker the hold of society on the person and the more daring and risk taking he is. The optimum distance is about 1–2mm; this gives freedom but indicates the person is not reckless. Such a person is the adventurous type who jumps out of aeroplanes to take photographs. When the distance is greater,

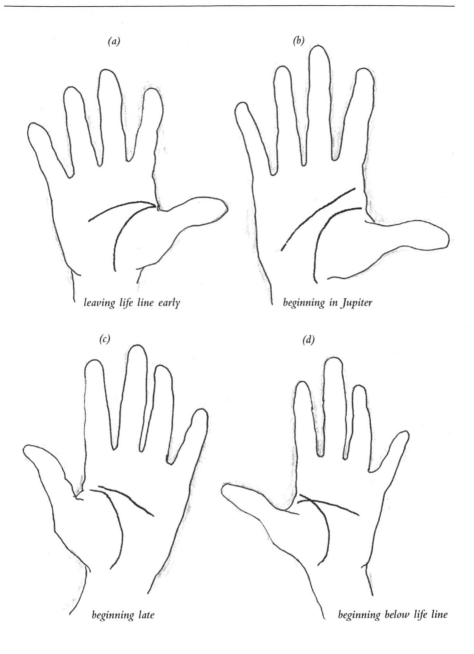

(a)

leaving life line early

(b)

beginning in Jupiter

(c)

beginning late

(d)

beginning below life line

Fig. 3.9 Head Lines I

recklessness, daredevilry and possibly antisocial behaviour are present. Morality imposes no restraint, which is good because it means greater freedom is possible. However, often the person steps beyond boundaries and hurts people. So you must be careful when relating with such a person. I have not seen any studies on psychopaths, but it would be very interesting to know what type of head lines they have.

Sometimes the head and life line start and run for a short distance together before the head line suddenly jumps up and becomes independent. *See fig. 3.9a*. This is a good sign, showing that in this life steps are being taken to become more mature, independent and conscious, although connection with family and society is still present.

Sometimes a head line begins in the mount of Jupiter. *See fig. 3.9b*. This is an indication of an exceptional mind, one that can be successful and influence groups of people. Often political leaders and company directors have this type of line. When it is very strong and straight, running down into the mount of Lunar, it is an indication of a very great person.

Often when the head line is separate, it also begins late. *See fig. 3.9c*. This does not indicate mental disability; rather, it means that the person has entered into the ego at an age later than normal. This is a blessing, for it gives more experience, usually on an unconscious level, of what it means to live beyond mind and personality – in other words, to be enlightened. It is very important to discuss this with the holder, because most people are not conscious that they have qualities of perception that are special. To confirm this, ask the person what is the earliest age he can remember. Often he can't remember anything before the age of five. This is also a good question to ask when you see a problem at the beginning of the life line. Often this person too can't remember anything before five years of age. In this case it is because of repression, but in the former case it is because there was no ego present who remembers. A late-starting head line indicates that a person has been working on himself in other lives. This denotes a person who is consciously trying to expand or raise his level of consciousness, usually by following a spiritual practice, by associating with a spiritual master or by doing good work.

When the head line begins below the life line in the mount of Mars, it is not a good sign. *See fig. 3.9d*. Mental problems and destructive thinking patterns are present and there is usually a history of mental illness in the family. Diseases of the central nervous system can also be indicated.

As with the life line, when the head line begins beyond the front edge of the palm it means excess. The person who possesses this feature usually has a very active mind, difficult to turn off. He is always difficult to relate to over a long period, and he can lose it mentally if external pressures become too much. This is especially true if the heart line also starts beyond the front edge of the palm. All the subjects I've seen with such beginnings have had mental collapses which entailed them being hospitalised for some time.

When the head and life line are separate, it is an indication the subject does not have a fear-based personality. If there are indications of anger, the person is anger based (numbers 1, 2 and 9 on the enneagram).

Positive mount of Mars

Before leaving this area of the palm, I want to discuss the positive (+) mount of Mars. *See fig. 3.10.* This mount of Mars is located above the mount of Venus, below the life line and bordered, towards the centre of the palm, by the life line as well.

The (+) mount of Mars is associated with power. It is masculine. There is a correlation between the mount of Mars and the subject's relationship (or lack of one) with the father, and a correlation with the subject's direct relationship with power. This area gives information about aggression and past-life involvement with aggression. No marks or lines on the (+) mount of Mars is an indication of health around issues of power, and also an indication that the relationship with the father is good, unless other aspects indicate problems.

When marks are present on the (+) mount of Mars it shows that issues with power and with the father are present. When marks are present in both hands, an issue has been carried over from other lives. Lines on the mount of Mars in the passive hand mean past-life involvement with aggression. Usually the person was the aggressor, who did all sorts of nasty things, especially as a soldier. Funnily enough, I see this more often in women's hands than in men's.

Often the active hand contains fewer markings on the (+) mount of Mars. This shows that a person is resolving past-life karma, very often incarnating only for this purpose. As an aside, it is interesting to note that at the time of writing I am visiting a spiritual ashram where almost every person has these markings, especially the women.

Lines coming up from the mount of Mars that cross the life line can have different meanings. First, they show that development with the father is deficient. The father usually is not available or is not giving love. Often the father has physically and/or sexually abused the child. Inquire gently about this, for it is a sensitive issue. With women, when these marks are present it shows they have problems with embodiment, with owning and sitting in their own power. They usually feel inadequate about themselves. In men, it usually shows as physical abuse and/or difficulties assuming the role of being a man. However, I only seem to discuss this point with women, and I don't know why.

Second, an upward slashing line from the mount of Mars can mean a major accident or a serious disease where the person almost dies. This is always a strong karmic event or, let's say, a debt to be paid.

Category 2

Category 2 refers to the way the head line runs across the palm. There are many ways in which it can do this.

Head line running straight across the palm (*fig. 3.8c*)

A head line running straight across the palm indicates a mental channel that is using average intelligence. This channel of intelligence focuses mainly on the outer physical world. I define average intelligence as awareness of the world through the senses, relying mostly on logic. In this channel 2 plus 2 really equals 4. And the straighter the line, the more single-pointed the perceptions. Subjects with this line tackle the world like an arrow shooting at a target. They are well suited for organising and completing goals.

Ideas have a strong tendency to become set and fixed in this type of person's mind, he finds it difficult to change. The keeper of this line has to be really convinced before he changes his mind. He wants to know how a conclusion has

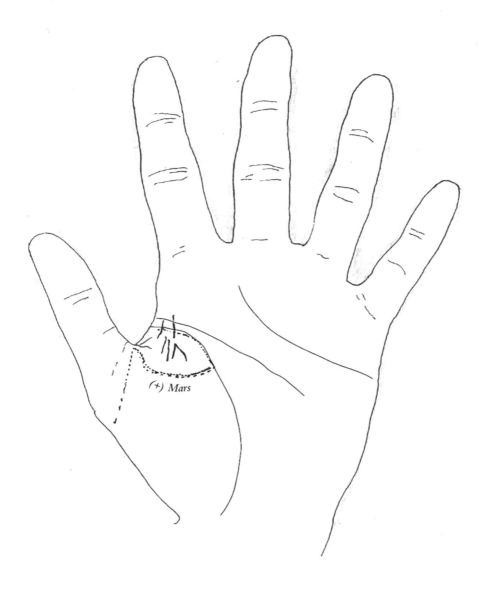

Fig. 3.10 (+) Mount of Mars, Showing Markings

been arrived at and is not satisfied unless the steps involved are clearly shown.

The longer the line, the more fixed the ideas can be. If the line runs right to the end of the palm, you can be sure that narrow-mindedness and stubbornness are present and the person is like a horse with blinkers. If the line is short, intensity is more likely to be present.

If this line starts in the mount of Jupiter and goes straight down like a rocket, you have a person who is quite special, usually influencing large groups of people either politically or spiritually. He may be found in business, but this is not as prevalent as the other cases.

When the head line runs straight across the palm I look to see if there is flexibility in other places, for example in the thumb. If the tip of the thumb bends back fairly easily, it shows flexibility of action. If the thumb is stiff, it shows inflexibility of action. I also bend back the tips of the fingers. If these are also stiff, we are talking serious inflexibility.

As an aside, if all the fingers are very flexible, it means the subject is too easily influenced and this will always be an issue in his life. A little firmness from Saturn is good to keep the balance. A person must have some idea of who he is in the world, what his boundaries are and what is good for him. Some firmness in Saturn gives these qualities.

Head line curving into the mount of Lunar (*fig. 3.8d*)
When the head line has a slight curve but does not go deeply into the Lunar mount, I consider it to be a channel of average intelligence. Most people have this line and I don't say much about it. Sometimes it's good to be just average, not special. All the mental abilities are present and can be used and enjoyed. Maybe there are no great talents, but so what? This is better than having a malfunctioning head line. Such a head line shows intuition and creativity, but the person is not as centred in the intuitive as he would be if he had a curving intuitive head line.

When the head line dips or curves into the lunar area, we have the intuitive head line. Sensitivity, creativity and intuition are its key attributes. The main focus of a person with this channel is the inner worlds. The deeper the dip into the lunar area, the stronger the attributes and the more deeply a person can enter into the collective unconscious – which can be compared to a sea of bottomless thoughts, dreams and ideas contained in the universal mind.

When the head line dips very deeply into the mount of Lunar and runs parallel, or almost parallel, with the life line, we have what is called 'the writer's line'. *See fig. 3.11a*. And most often this is true. The person is very creative, very sensitive and very expressive. Unfortunately most people with this type of line commit suicide! You can be certain that a person with a deeply dipping head line will suffer periodically from depression. There will be no external reason for the depression, even though he will identify one. It is just part of the internal package. In fact, depression is a factor with all types of intuitive head lines. It is important to discuss depression with all the types and to stress that during periods of depression they must make no important decisions or take major action. Learning meditation to witness the depression should be advised.

Depression is a high price to pay for creative and intuitive abilities. The more sensitive a person is, the more he is affected by the vast wasteland of the collective unconscious, which contains mostly old dreams, nightmares, bizarre thoughts and weird feelings. A sensitive person needs some protection from this or else he becomes a wreck.

With a dipping intuitive head line, the person is centred in the creative dream world. When used creatively, this deep centredness can be very positive and beautiful. On the negative side, a person centred in this world who has no reliable check on reality is going to suffer from both an inability to see reality clearly and self-delusion.

General characteristics

When the head line splits and branches, with one branch continuing straight while the other dips into the Lunar, it means a person has a channel in two worlds, the dream and the so-called physical, real world. *See fig. 3.11b*. This can be great because the person can balance the physical world with the inner world of imagination. Such people are usually good storytellers because they have the ability to enter the inner worlds and then return to the outer worlds and speak clearly about them. However, if development in Mercury has not been correct,

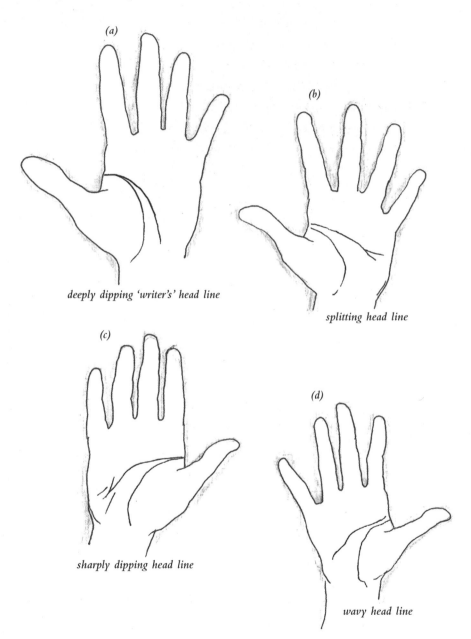

(a)

deeply dipping 'writer's' head line

(b)

splitting head line

(c)

sharply dipping head line

(d)

wavy head line

Fig. 3.11   Head Lines II

this balance is upset and there is stronger belief in the dream worlds and difficulty in distinguishing dreams from everyday awareness.

When the Mercury finger is bent and the head line is split, there is a 95 per cent certainty that there are problems in distinguishing dreams from reality. If you ask these people to describe an event that happened only five minutes ago, the story will be totally different from what actually happened. Everyone does this to some extent, but in this case there is a psychological need to present the story to themselves in a form they can accept and that corresponds with their image of themselves. A bent finger of Mercury with a non-splitting, dipping head line can also show this quality of distorting the truth. However, in this case the person does it more or less consciously. He suffers from self-delusions and lies to cover up his feelings of inadequacy. It is not easy to have a deeply dipping head line.

Sometimes the head line runs straight and then dips sharply into the lunar area. *See fig. 3.11c.* This shows a person who initially has a normal interest in the physical world and then switches his interest to the inner or spiritual world. Often a sudden experience turns his focus 180 degrees inwards.

At the end of the head line sometimes you will see small, separated lines branching off. This means late development of talents. *See fig. 3.11c.*

Lines starting on the head line and going up usually refer to a channel of interest and associated abilities. What the interest is depends on which mount the line points to: if towards Mercury, there is interest in writing, communication or business; if towards the Sun, a creative, artistic channel and interest are present. 'Interest' is the key word.

A strong head line means full force, full passion, and a strong mental body. A strong head line can overcome weakness in the life line. It is said that the head line rather than the life line indicates how long the life will be. (I mention this about the head line quite often, because people get scared when they see that their life line is broken or short. Death and fear of death are always an issue, whether expressed or not.) Short head lines in both hands can mean premature death. I have not verified this, as I have not made a point of looking at recently dead bodies. A strong, passionate head line is also associated with anger. Check the mount of Mars and the thumb. A person with a passionate head line needs an outlet, such as a sport, to vent pent-up energy and feelings.

Persons with short head lines are usually intense and lead action-packed lives. They may go out quickly, but they do so intensely. Whatever they need to do in this life, they do quickly, using up their life force. On occasions you may see on the passive hand (usually the left) a short head line and a diffused life line and on the active hand (usually the right) a normal life and head line. People with this combination have lived short past lives. Ask them what they feel about dying and death, and go from there.

When the head line is wavy, a person will tend to think in a wavering manner. *See fig. 3.11d.* Sometimes it is difficult for him to go straight from A to B; he must go via C, for example. He gets there but not directly. Also, he sometimes has difficulty seeing the light at the end of the tunnel. So doubt and frustration can be present. It is good for this person to step back and get an overview of what he is doing. Wavy head lines can also mean periods of confusion.

A pale or faint head line tells you the person has less force to work with, or is keeping it hidden, or is using it in a refined and ethereal way. Check the other aspects showing life force. Refined people usually have refined hands. There is a particular look to them.

When the head line becomes thinner it means less mental energy is present during that period. Thickenings in the head line mean the opposite. These are good periods for projects.

Breaks in the head line are not good, especially if they occur early on. They signify mental defects or breakdown in the ability to function clearly. For example, the ability to concentrate, to sustain mental activity and attain goals is weak. Fogginess, confusion, anxiety, inability to make decisions and inability to learn can all be indicated. In particular, breaks early in the head line mean defects in the central nervous system, resulting in nervous disorders such as a tic or even epilepsy. In addition, if there are slashing lines coming from the mount of Mars, it can mean head injuries. *See fig. 3.10.*

Gaps in the head line are rare. Anything can happen during a gap – enlightenment, death, or nothing. However, the potential for 'tripping the light fantastic' is high at this time.

If there is a tassel at the end of the head line, it means dissipation of mental energy. *See fig. 3.12a.*

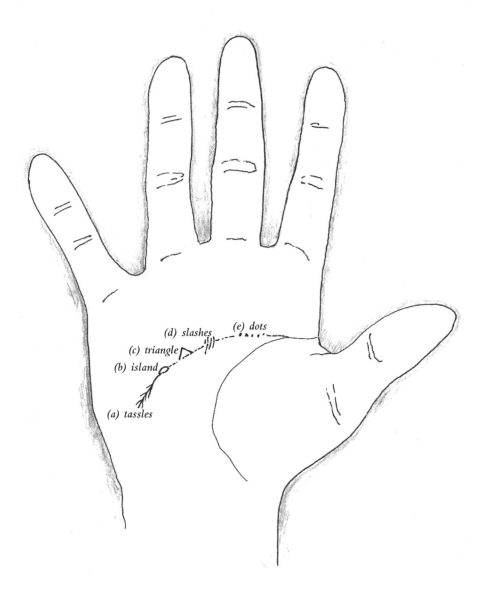

Fig. 3.12 Special Markings on the Head Line

Islands on the line always mean weak periods when full power is split. *See fig. 3.12b*.

A triangle on the head line means an energy boost, but triangles are rare. *See fig. 3.12c*.

Lots of small dots or markings on the head line mean some problem with the central nervous system. *See fig. 3.12e*. Again, confusion and/or headaches and/or weakness and anxiety are present. These persons are likely to have nervous diseases. Often I find I have to probe the subject to find out where the problem is. Marks on both hands indicate genetic disease.

Branching at the end of the head line means multi-interests and is a good sign.

If the head line becomes fainter and thinner, this can be a sign that someone is not utilising his full mental potential. He is not putting his entire consciousness into the mental body. When there is an acutely dipping intuitive line, I can understand that the person doesn't want to be fully aware of all the muck in the collective unconscious, even though he will miss finding the lotus growing out of it. Often a person with a fading head line feels frustrated in the realisation of his potential, and it helps to point this out and discuss it. This applies to all fading lines. You must remember that a person having a reading wants to hear a specific message. Sometimes it doesn't matter if the reading is incomplete. It's amazing how the important message comes out when it needs to.

Excess at the beginning and ending of lines is not good. A head line running right to the end of the palm accents the traits of that line. Usually it conveys fixations, stubbornness and the person's inability to see more than his own viewpoint. This can be an advantage however; extreme single-mindedness in Papaji's hand helped him to bring people to enlightenment.

When there are Xs between the life line and head line, it means litigation, land disputes and/or family disputes.

I don't know why, but I always try to see aspects, events and traits in a very general way. Sometimes, details are fascinating, but I am more interested in underlying, general themes. I have short fingers, so maybe that is why. Usually when I give a reading the person will say, 'I must tell you that I was with another reader (not a palmist) who told me in detail what you are talking about generally.' And often I am told that the points I make are the same as those made in an astrology reading. You don't have to follow my approach. You can gear your readings so that more emphasis is placed on knowing details.

HEART LINE
'How Do You Love?'

The heart line begins under Mercury, runs across the palm and ends in one of the four areas listed below. It runs in the opposite direction to the head line and life line. The heart line is similar to the head line in that there are four basic types, determined by where the heart line ends:

- under Saturn finger
- between Saturn and Jupiter fingers
- on the base of the Jupiter finger
- in the middle of the mount of Jupiter

The heart line, like the thumb, can be set high or low. A high-set heart line shows a good separation between heart and head line. *See fig. 3.13.* This person tends to have a cheerful, sunny disposition. With a low-set heart line, the person tends to be depressed and gloomy. Because a low-set heart line is closer to the head line and the lines are running in opposite directions, there is interference. *See fig. 3.14.* This friction uses up energy, and the closeness of the mind also influences the heart. All this can make for a gloomy person who may well suffer from a 'midlife crisis'. When the heart and head line are running close together, the mind becomes muddled with emotions, and emotions are distracted by thoughts. A good separation of the heart and head line is important for clear functioning of the emotional and mental body. Perhaps the person with a high-set heart line is happier, because he is more distanced from the mind.

Often you see lines running from the heart to the head line or from the head to the heart line. In the former it means the heart is influencing the head, and in the latter the head is influencing the heart. Either way, this is not a good sign.

A wide and deep heart line showing an intense red colour indicates strong energy and passion.

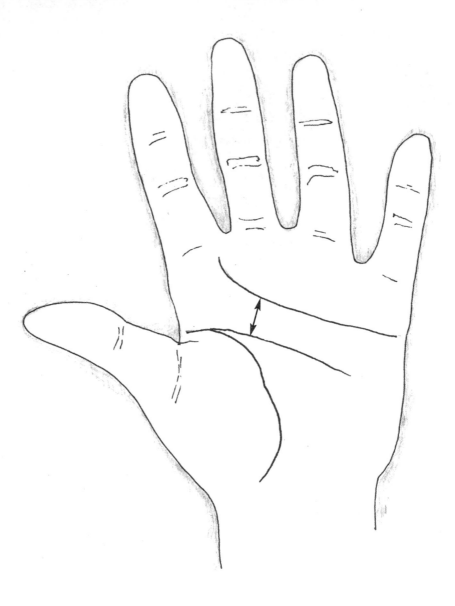

Fig. 3.13 Good Separation of Heart and Head Line

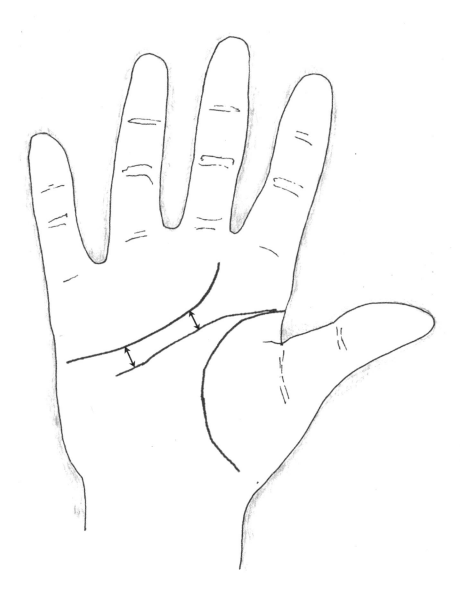

Fig. 3.14 Heart and Head Line Close Together
'Midlife Crisis'

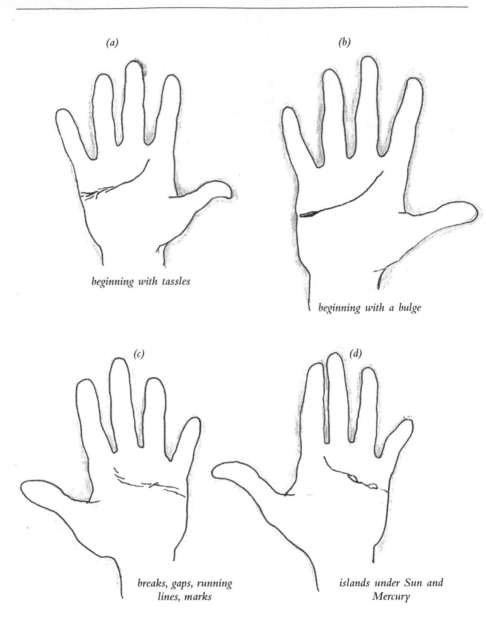

(a)

beginning with tassles

(b)

beginning with a bulge

(c)

breaks, gaps, running lines, marks

(d)

islands under Sun and Mercury

Fig. 3.15 Heart Lines I

The best functioning heart line has no breaks, marks or islands. This heart line is very rare. Almost everyone has some breaks or weaknesses. In fact, the heart line always shows the most breaks and discontinuity.

The beginning of the heart line is very important because it shows the initial relationship with the mother. It tells if the person was a wanted child; how much the mother loved the baby at the time of conception, during the first six months of pregnancy and at the time of birth. There can also be indications of problems at birth and what the emotional and/or physical condition of the mother was during the birth. There is much information to be gained from this one spot on the palm. If another person takes on the role of mother, as a nanny for example, this registers as a line coming into the heart line.

The child's initial relationship with the mother is so important because it sets the pace at which his emotional body will grow and determines how strong it will be. Most later problems associated with the heart – physically and emotionally – can be traced back to this early relationship with the mother.

The heart line should begin on the front of the palm. If it starts behind the palm, some emotional excess is present. This can also be an indication of possible serious genetic disease involving the auto-immune system.

A good start to the heart line is full and straight with no breaks or tassels. This means that the mother's love was present and the child was wanted and loved in at least the first six months of pregnancy. In this instance, the person receives in full the power needed for the emotional body to grow. You would be surprised how rare it is to see a good heart line beginning.

When the beginning of the heart line is tasselled, it means the mother's love was not available and the child was unwanted. *See fig. 3.15a*. If the line is thin and weak, it shows that not much care was given, even if the mother did love the baby. For example, she may have been sick and unable to provide for the child.

If the beginning of the heart line bulges (appears thicker), it means that love was present but was possibly excessive or expressed in a neurotic way, or that the mother was not capable of giving love because of either a physical condition or an emotional reason. See *fig. 3.15b*. Any markings on the line at this point indicate an affliction or illness of mother or child, a problem with the mother-child relationship, and/or adverse environmental influences. Ask the subject questions in order to pinpoint the situation.

When the beginning of the heart line is distressed on both hands, it indicates the repeated choosing of an incarnation that does not result in the proper growth of the emotional body. But this is a karmic process that must be completed on its own accord. Nothing can be done to help. When it is seen in only one hand, usually the active hand, there is a possibility the fault can be corrected through discipline, wisdom or understanding. This point is true also for the other primary lines when they are distressed in both hands.

As an aside to this, I have noticed that the beginnings of my heart line and life line have improved significantly in recent years. They are both stronger and less tasselled and are generally in better shape. The only reason I can give for this is that as I have worked on myself, becoming more conscious, letting go of emotional and mental garbage, these lines have restructured themselves. There is no doubt that my capacity to love, to remain open to love, and to accept a person more unconditionally has greatly increased, at least in the moment. So, it makes sense that the channels have changed. I used to think that the beginning of the heart line was fixed, since it is a past event. However, this does not seem to be the case.

Here is a physical example of the future influencing the past. Sometimes when I meditate I fall into the remembrance of some time in the past when I was regularly sitting in a particular place. I then find myself sending energy to that past time. I always wonder if the future could change the past, as suggested by many of Kurt Vonnegut's books.

The best heart line is one that starts high, has no breaks, gaps or islands, and is strong and continuous. Somewhere near Saturn, it begins to curve upwards and then ends at the base of the Jupiter finger (but does not enter into it). Entering into the finger would again mean excess. This line shows that the person has a strong, emotional body and is capable of love, both passionate and higher spiritual love. This person can be compassionate and love unconditionally. On the physical plane, the circulatory system is sound, as is the digestive system and eyesight. There is a direct correlation between the strength of the heart line and these physical organs. A weak heart line indicates problems with the circulatory system. These people usually die of strokes and heart disease.

People with other types of heart lines can love unconditionally and be compassionate, but not as freely and effortlessly. To determine a person's degree of compassion, check the setting of the thumb. The lower the thumb the more giving and compassionate a person is.

An island on the heart line under Mercury means gastrointestinal weakness. An island under the Sun means eyesight problems and a probability of injuries to the eyes. See *fig. 3.15d*. A person might not be ill, but a potential weakness is there. Whether symptoms appear depends on factors such as lifestyle and temperament.

On the heart line you can find the most breaks and gaps. See *fig. 3.15c*. Ancillary lines are often seen running down towards the head line. See *fig. 3.17b*. I guess affairs of the heart are the toughest and cause the most pain.

Little lines coming and going from the heart line can mean many love affairs – the heart energy is going out to someone. It is best when other lines do not cross them; this would mean trouble in relationships.

Breaks and gaps and run-on lines all indicate weakness. These people are sensitive and can be easily hurt. They don't have the strength to ward off intense emotional input from others in the form of insults or criticism, and they cannot handle the ups and downs of relationships.

On the physical level, a weak heart line indicates problems with the circulatory system. These people usually die of strokes and heart disease. Check where the heart line begins. If beyond the palm, and starting lower, it can mean diseases of the cardiovascular system. Check to see which line is weaker, the heart or the head. This indicates which types of disease a person is likely to get. Look for little marks running along the heart line. This is a good indication of circulatory weakness. If there are many little marks on the heart line and head line, it means that the immune system is weak and the person must take extra care. Most people want to know how and from what they will die.

The four types of heart line endings

1 Under Saturn (*fig. 3.16a*)

The heart line ending under Saturn is characterised by the need for relationship. There is a basic longing to be with the other. Often persons with this heart

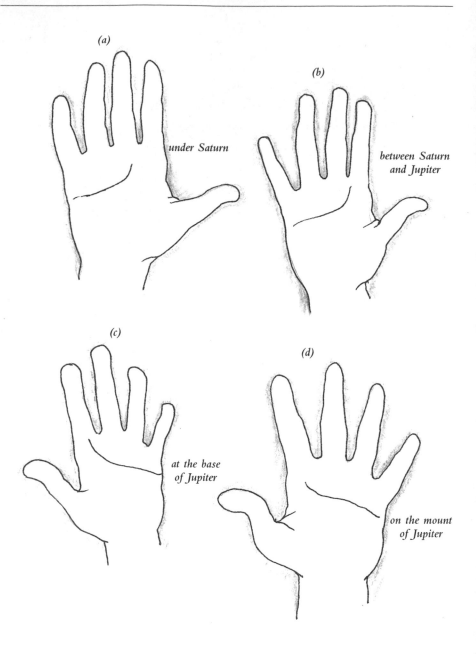

(a)

under Saturn

(b)

*between Saturn
and Jupiter*

(c)

*at the base
of Jupiter*

(d)

*on the mount
of Jupiter*

Fig. 3.16 Heart Line Endings

line need the other to see and experience God, and in general do not feel complete unless they are in relationship. People with this type of line can experience love and compassion, but they go through periods when they are not in touch with their feelings, when they feel almost blank. They can be distant and have problems going deeply into love, more often staying on the sensual and practical side. Often these people are very sexual and passionate. In a relationship they need a lot of trust, and flower when they find someone they do trust.

It appears that a heart line ending under Saturn is not complete. It is better for the heart to rise out of Saturn. Further development of the emotional channel is needed. Very often, secondary sister lines and/or a Girdle of Venus will develop to handle the emotional channel's need to rise to higher levels.

The heart line ending under Saturn is concerned mainly with ego gratification. Even the person's compassion can originate from the need for ego gratification. The influence of Saturn is always to regulate, to be the watchdog, the moral judge. It is concerned with the mind and duality, with trying to control and regulate the human condition. Saturn in excess is mostly a drag. It makes the person gloomy and repressed and keeps him fixed on self-gratification.

If Saturn is weak, the person does not have a sufficient sense of himself, of what is right and wrong for him. Saturn provides the moral foundation the ego needs to stand on. Saturn is needed for earth grounding, patience, and sense of self and morality. Love needs to fly higher and go beyond these limitations, and this is the reason there is trouble with this type of heart line.

2 Between Saturn and Jupiter (fig. 3.16b)

A heart line that rises after Saturn and ends between Saturn and Jupiter indicates the person is cool in love. Type-2 heart lines are generally not ruled by passion and the person usually does not fall head over heels in love. This person may practise tantra and enjoy using the love/sex energy to reach higher states of consciousness. He may also enjoy sitting for hours with his partner and doing breathing exercises in some controlled way. To a certain degree, persons with this type of heart line exhibit signs of dispassion and coolness, and there is again some degree of selfishness or focus on self-gratification.

3 At the base of Jupiter (*fig. 3.16c*)

After Saturn the heart line begins to rise towards Jupiter. Jupiter represents higher spiritual ideals, and it is good when the heart line rises into it.

This area of the heart line represents higher spiritual love. It brings love out of the realm of desire, enabling a person to love unconditionally and also to know the love of one's spiritual self, which has no address of you and me. Compassion towards others comes into play with this type of heart line as well. All heart lines that end after Saturn have these qualities. The easiest and clearest flowing channel is one ending at the base of the Jupiter finger. This is the full heart line, type 3. A full heart line shows true development of the soul, in that there has been a turning away from mere ego gratification. Some form of selflessness is present. A full heart line with a good low-set thumb is an excellent indication of a very loving and caring soul. Basically a type-3 heart line is complete; the major work on the heart is finished. The person can experience and give his all if needed and desired. However, when there are weaknesses in the line, such as breaks, gaps and islands, there is still minor work to be done.

4 In the mount of Jupiter (*fig. 3.16d*)

The last type of heart line rises after Saturn and ends somewhere in the middle of the mount of Jupiter. This line has a special meaning. The mount of Jupiter is concerned with goals and ambitions. When the heart line ends here it is very important that love is infused into the person's goals and ambitions. The more prevalent the love, the more content the person feels. This means that in the pursuit of interests, projects and careers, the person's main motivation should be love – doing something he loves and/or giving a service where love is involved. When the main motivation is love, he is most content. When it is not love but desire of money or power, the goal can still be achieved but is not as gratifying. A job should not be taken just for money, prestige or survival. If this line is in both hands, it is very important for the person to do service because this need is the primary consideration.

This kind of heart line shows that there is a special ability to transmit love energy through a medium, be it massage or design or whatever. Often persons with this special talent are not aware that they have it. It is good to spend some time discussing this.

Nanaguru, an Indian guru whose 'job' it is to transmit love, has this heart line in both hands; and really, it is the only interesting point in his hand, the rest is just average. It seems he is here only to transmit love and nothing else.

The angle at which the heart line rises after Saturn can vary from slight to acute. Persons with an acute rising heart line are passionate, get excited easily and fall in love very quickly.

At the end of the heart line there can be branches. *See fig. 3.17a*. When this occurs, a person is able to love and be loving to more than one person at a time. He can easily fall in love with many people. He mainly interacts through love. When love is not present, he is easily distracted and withdraws quickly. If love is not present, he is not interested, even if it means material losses or loss of friendships.

Sometimes one branch goes to the mount of Jupiter while the other rises to the base of Jupiter. This means that service has only partial importance. Higher spiritual love or concern with the unfolding of the person's higher consciousness is at least as important. One branch can be stronger or they can be of equal size, width and strength. When branches are present in both hands and the service line is weaker, I would advise the person to withdraw from service and devote himself to his own enlightenment. Having this line in both hands indicates something carried over from other lives. At this stage the person needs to drop service and focus completely on self-realisation.

A branch running down from the heart line to the beginning of the life line is not a good sign. *See fig. 3.17d*. It means loss of heart. There are problems and real difficulties in relationships with the opposite sex, and usually the person shows characteristics of the opposite sex. If it is in both hands, many books state that the person will die a sudden death. I have had no confirmation of this as yet, but I do use this information and pass it on to people. If there is no indication of loss at the end of the life line, it is as good a guess as any that death will be sudden. And funnily enough, people don't mind hearing this. Mostly they say. 'Yes, that feels right.'

Little lines leaving the heart line again tell of losses of energy, but in this

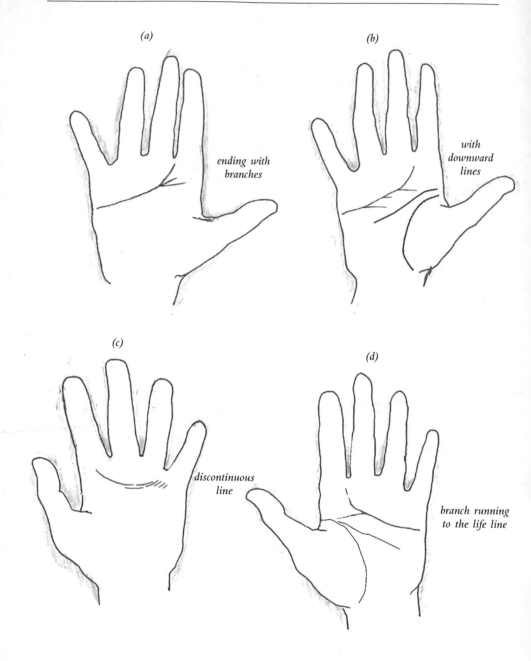

Fig. 3.17   Heart Lines II

instance it usually means the person's heart goes out to someone, not necessarily in a detrimental way. Many small lines are, of course, a drain on the channel. And a large number of downward lines means too much sensitivity, the heart going out to others too readily, a tendency to be easily influenced. When these lines go down to the head line and join it, the heart is influencing the head. It means emotions are a factor in decision-making and need to be taken into consideration in order to arrive at a satisfactory conclusion.

When a line leaves the heart line, crosses with another line and forms an X, we are looking at relationships that don't work out or are difficult and show a strong negative interaction. These situations are usually the result of karma and need to be played out.

Once in a while I see a heart line that is discontinuous. *See fig. 3.17c.* It is shown by a series of slashes running together. This means the person feels love or has interest in something for a while and then the love or interest just stops. He can't really be relied on and finds it difficult to feel content because of the many gaps. This discontinuity makes for unreliability of feelings, with often the holder going from one project to the next. This person needs a strong and caring maternal partner to help ground him.

Many dots and marks on the heart line mean heart and circulation problems. When these dots and marks are seen on the head line as well, it means that the immune system is weak. Along the heart line there can be thickening and thinning of the line. Thick areas indicate juicy periods of love, and thin areas periods when love and relations are sparse. This does not necessarily mean a negative period, for it might be a period of meditation and inner journeys. Weakness in the lines always means increased sensitivity and vulnerability.

Sometimes the head and heart line endings become thin and faint. Again, this shows the person is not applying full consciousness to the higher realms of heart and mind.

Chapter 4

SECONDARY LINES

Secondary lines do not always appear on the palm but they are as important as primary lines. The functioning of a person is not hindered by the absence of these lines; in fact, in some cases, it can be an advantage not to have them. For example, often it is better not to have a line of liver or a destiny line.

In general, secondary lines change and reform quicker and more often than primary lines. It is always important to remember that the lines and mounts are not static but dynamic, changing as we do through the experience of life.

GIRDLE OF VENUS
'Love One Another'

Associated with the heart line is the secondary line called the Girdle of Venus. *See fig. 4.1.* The Girdle of Venus, a sister line to the heart line, comes into play when the heart channel is not sufficient to carry the heart load — for example, when the heart line ends at Saturn, which is usually when a Girdle of Venus is present. A Girdle of Venus can also come into play when the heart channel is weak and full of leaks.

The Girdle of Venus ends at the base between Jupiter and Saturn and starts somewhere in the middle of the palm. A full Girdle of Venus (gv) starts between the bases of Mercury and the Sun finger, but usually the gv is modified and can start anywhere. There can also be more than one modified gv. *See fig. 4.2.*

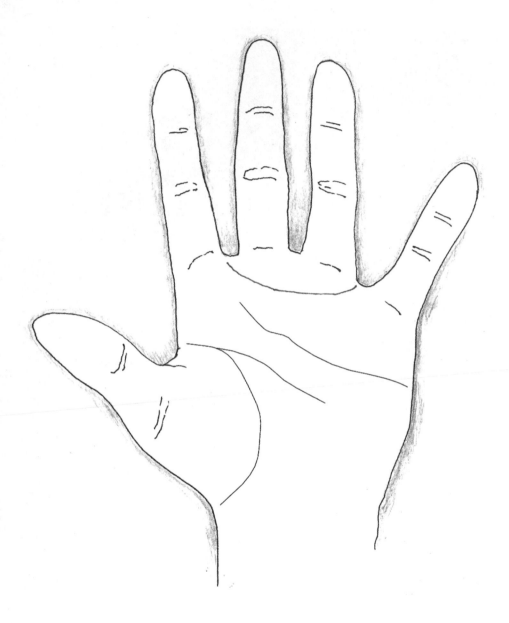

Fig. 4.1 Girdle of Venus

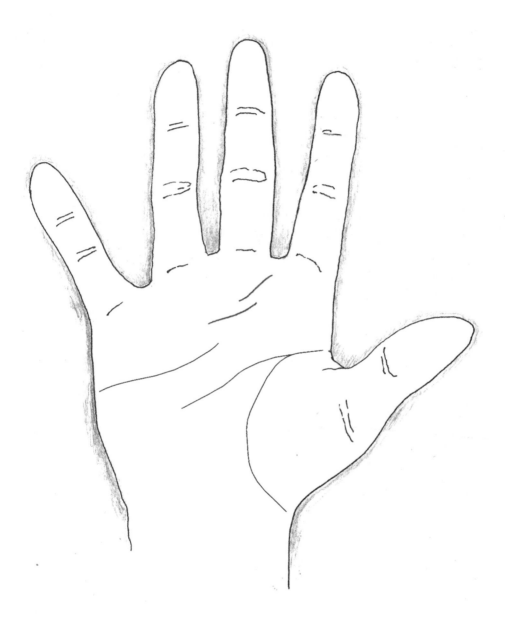

Fig. 4.2 Modified Girdle of Venus

Another situation where a gv is often present is when the heart line shuts down or retracts. This shutdown can be identified by comparing the hands. With a right-handed person, it can be that the heart line is shorter in the active right hand. With a left-handed person, the shutdown is more difficult to identify, for the active hand is not automatically the left hand.

In the palmistry books of 200 years ago, a gv meant 'nymphomaniac'. In modern times, we would not say that. Instead we would say that the gv increases the sensitivity and sensuality of its holder. Also it can just act as a sister line to the heart line. This is mostly true when the heart line ends in Saturn. People with a gv usually do have a strong sexual appetite, especially if they are not open to the higher aspects of love. They will instead channel the heart energy into sexuality.

Speaking of sexual energy, the development of the mount of Venus is important. A good mount shows strong energy. On the mount of Venus there can be horizontal lines coming across the mount from the thumb. If there are vertical lines crossing as well, it indicates strong sexual energy. *See fig. 4.3.* Mostly I've found this to be true.

These lines coming across the mount are an indication of excess energy or energy that is not being used or manifested. These lines are sometimes called 'worry lines'. Usually people possessing them are hyperactive, although it doesn't necessarily mean anxiety is present.

A small strong line located near the middle of the thumb and running across the middle of the mount of Venus means strong dependency on the opposite sex. *See fig. 4.3a.* I've usually found this line to be accurate.

SATURN LINE
'The Middle Way'

The Saturn line is known as the fortune or balance line. It is also known as the destiny line. *See figs. 4.4 and 4.5.* It is known as the fortune line because it shows the balance between what life brings to a person, his assets, and how he is able to use these assets to meet the challenges of life.

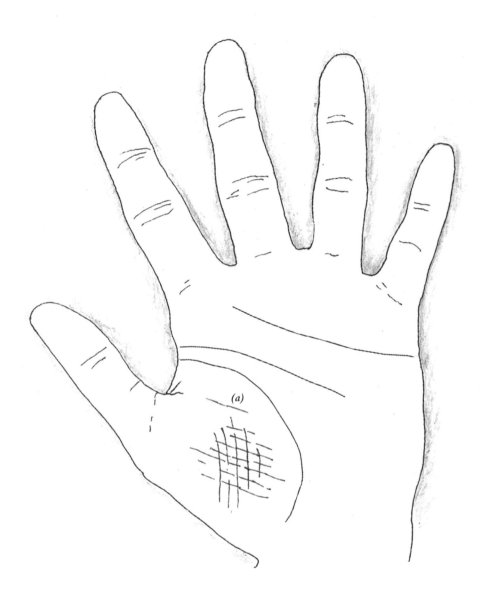

(a)

Fig. 4.3 Mount of Venus

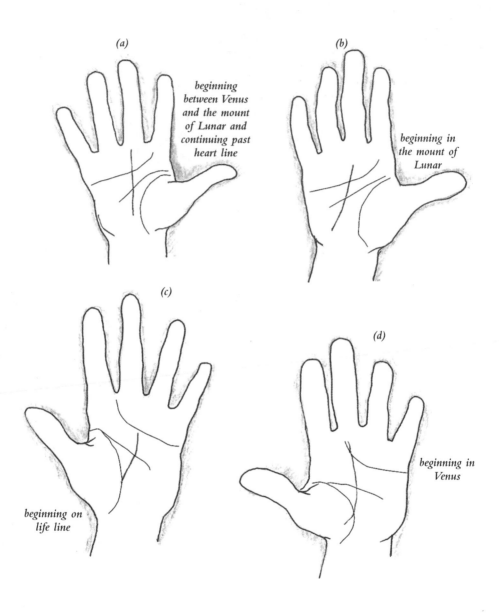

Fig. 4.4 Saturn Lines I

This line is a destiny line in as much as it fixes the life path. When the line is strong and clear, the person has a strong destiny. This does not always mean that the person has good fortune. The first time I saw a very strong Saturn line in the hand of a person I knew didn't have good fortune, I was shocked and taken aback. Then I realised that the Saturn line means *primarily destiny with fortune arising from the circumstances of destiny.*

In practice, however, a strong Saturn line usually does indicate a good fortune.

The Saturn line starts at the bottom of the palm, rises up towards Saturn and can end anywhere. The Saturn line can begin from several areas, with each one having a specific meaning. The area indicates the source of a person's powers and what he can rely on – in other words, the well from which he can draw water.

Before going on, I want to say that not having a strong Saturn line or not having one at all can be advantageous. It means that a person does not have a fixed destiny to be lived out. There is a degree of freedom and the possibility to determine his own path. And that is his destiny.

Having a strong, fixed Saturn line fixes the person's life into a definite pattern, which cannot be varied. In extreme cases even the raising of an arm is predetermined. For many it is preferable to have freedom rather than be caught in a fixed movie that must be played out, even if it means less material security.

As with other lines, breaks, gaps and islands indicate a weakness when misfortune can occur. A thickening or thinning of the line indicates a rich or lean period for the person. When there is a break and a new line starts before the old line is finished, this indicates a change of life direction – perhaps a change of career or other material change.

When the Saturn line begins directly below the Saturn finger at the base of the palm between the mount of Venus and the Lunar mount, it means the person's source of life force comes mainly from within his own deep inner core. *See fig. 4.4a*. In a crisis, when there is a real need to draw water from the well, he will find that he can draw on his own spirit, although some help may come from outside influences.

When the Saturn lines continues past the heart line, it is a good sign of fortune. *See fig. 4.4a.*

The Saturn line starting in the lunar area indicates spiritual work, either in

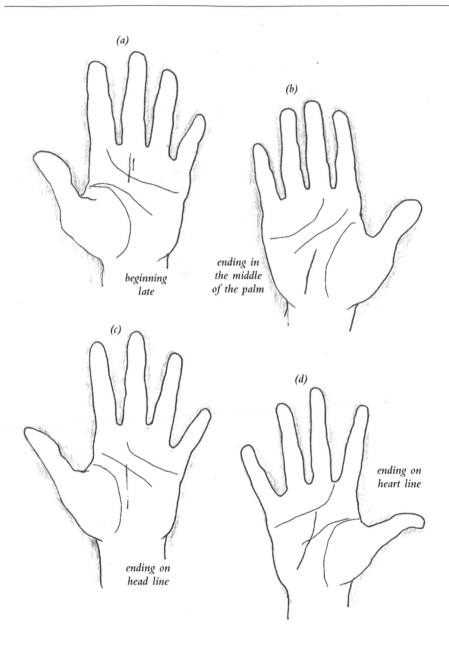

(a)

(b)

beginning late

ending in the middle of the palm

(c)

(d)

ending on heart line

ending on head line

Fig. 4.5 Saturn Lines II

past lives or this life. See *fig. 4.4b*. This means that there has been a direct experience of God, a knowledge that never leaves and can always be accessed. I tell people with this line that their knowledge of the nature of the universe is as valid as anyone else's and that they should trust their intuition in this regard. When the Saturn line starts in the lunar area, help will come from friends rather than family, and there will be spiritual help because of past spiritual work. The deeper in the lunar area the line starts, the deeper the person's connection with God. I call this line the 'hotline to God'. With this channel, the person can access and communicate with the higher realms. He can call upon them for strength and guidance. It is a good line to have and sometimes you will see more than one Saturn line showing additional past spiritual work and merit.

When the Saturn line begins on the life line, it means a strong connection to family and social mores. *See fig. 4.4c*. Committing acts that are frowned upon by society will be difficult. There will always be a family connection – in property or business as well as relationships. Help when needed will also come from family.

When the Saturn line starts within the mount of Venus behind the life line it means that the love energy of Venus helps the person and that his fortune is connected with creativity. *See fig. 4.4d*.

When a Saturn line starts late near the heart line or head line, it means late development of wealth. *See fig. 4.5a*.

The Saturn line can have several endings. When the Saturn line ends in the middle of the palm – which represents the deep unconscious, the unknown beyond form – it indicates that part of the person's destiny is to make, by himself, a discovery or realization. *See fig. 4.5b*. This can be the sign of the 'self-made' man.

When the line stops at the head line, it means that there will be losses due to incorrect judgements, false logic and delusions of the mind. *See fig. 4.5c*. I often tell these people to go with their gut feeling rather than logic when there is a pull between feelings and mind.

When the Saturn line stops at the heart line, there can be losses due to emotional reasons or love. *See fig. 4.5d*. For example, there can be large losses from loaning money to friends or lovers. To these people I say the opposite. If they do not want to lose their assets, they should be ruthlessly logical and strict with their decision.

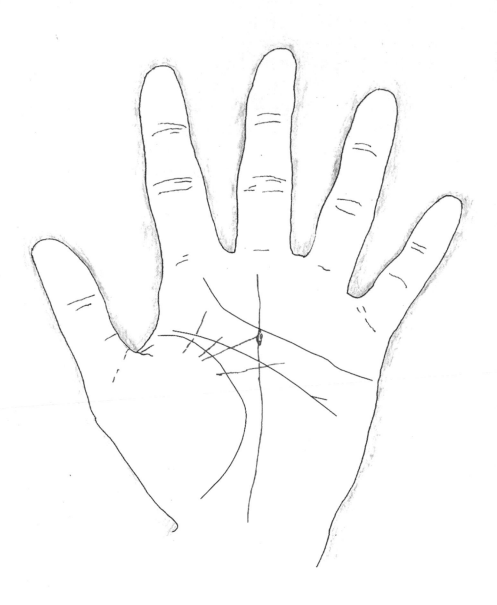

Fig. 4.6 Influence Lines Crossing the Saturn Line

Influence Lines

Lines crossing the Saturn line indicate influences on material matters, and they can be negative or positive.

When a line comes from the mount of Mars–Venus area, crosses the life line and intersects with the Saturn line it means a force is influencing fortune in a major way. *See fig. 4.6.* This force can be a person or a situation. If the line comes into an island, break or gap then it means loss of substantial wealth.

Influence lines are a strong indication of now, so it is good to pinpoint the influence in the life of the subject.

Influence lines that cross over from the mount of Mars and touch the other lines – Saturn, head line or heart line – show that a force is having a major influence during this time of the person's life. The influence can be positive or negative, of course. To determine this, look to see how the line ends. If the line enters into a weakness such as a break, gap or island, the influence is negative. If the line goes into strength, and the line remains strong or grows, it is a good influence.

An influence line can show how and in what direction a person's growth is heading and developing. I will give an example of this from my own hand. I have a strong influence line from the mount of Mars that crosses the life line, rising to the end of my heart line. At that point my heart line began to grow and now there is a small thin channel extending to the base of the Jupiter finger. My heart line originally ended at Saturn. I attribute this influence to my spiritual master. From being with my master over the years, my capacity to love has definitely increased. And this is reflected in my heart line. It was astonishing for me to see the heart line grow, merging with a modified gv. Under certain circumstances the girdle of Venus can even become a full-fledged heart line.

There seems to be a dominant influence line that indicates the direction of growth, in a way showing the karmic push. For example, the influence line going towards my heart line changed direction and started flowing into my head line. This was a time of mental growth. When that period was over, the line switched back to influence my heart line again. I have watched this occur several times over the last few years and each time my focus changed from affairs of the heart to mental activity, such as writing this book.

Squares and triangles

If the influence line ends inside a square, it means protection from the influence. Squares anywhere on the hand mean protection. They are good to have. *See fig. 5.1a.*

Triangles located on lines are thought to be a power boost to the line. Generally, I see them on the head line. *See fig. 5.1g.*

SUN LINE
'It's Light, It's Love, It's Creativity'

A Sun line, like the Saturn line, can start anywhere in the palm. In practice, I find that the Sun line usually starts in the middle of the palm or on the mount of Lunar. However, it clearly ends in the direction of the Sun finger. *See fig. 4.7a.* The Sun line is less common than the Saturn line. The Sun line indicates good fortune, light, creativity and love. Its fortune is of a higher and lighter value than the fortune of the Saturn line. It is a channel of light and a very good line to have. Very often I see a small Sun line that starts above the heart line and rises to the base of the Sun finger. *See fig. 4.7b.* This indicates love of fine art and aesthetic beauty and is usually also a sign that the person has some artistic talent. The line is a creative channel.

Sometimes I see a Sun line that is not a solid and straight line but is made up of several small faint lines, sometimes going in different directions. *See fig. 4.7c.* This means that a creative channel is present, but more as a potential. Actualisation can occur if the person focuses on creativity and applies consciousness to it. Then the line can become solid and straight. Often people with this type of line need to be told that they have creative potential channels, because they think they have no talent.

A line of Sun on only the passive hand can mean a dormant channel: one that is not in active use, or used only in a passive way, as for instance in the appreciation and love of art.

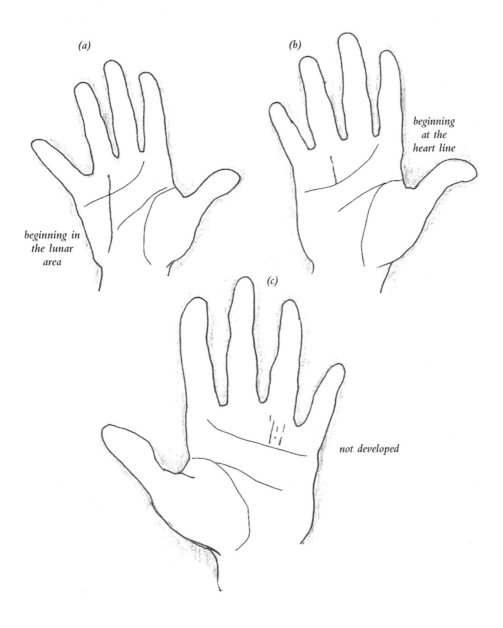

(a)

(b)

*beginning
at the
heart line*

*beginning in
the lunar
area*

(c)

not developed

Fig. 4.7 Sun Line

LINE OF LIVER
'Health Notice'

The line of liver starts at the bottom of the palm near the end of the life line. It then runs diagonally across and up the palm ending somewhere facing the direction of the mount of Mercury. *See fig. 4.8*. The liver line can show variation in length and thickness, and there can be several independent lines each referring to a different health issue.

The line of liver is concerned with health and vitality. This line has been related to success in business, because health and vitality are good assets for success.

There are different schools of thought concerning the line of liver, and this can lead to some confusion. Some authorities state that a good, strong, continuous line of liver means good health, vitality and success. Other authorities say it is better to have no line of liver at all, because the presence of a line of liver means that some health crisis has been present. I tend to agree with the latter view, but feel that the former can be valid in certain individuals. This illustrates the point that there are no black and white rules in hand analysis. In one hand a strong line of liver can mean good vitality, but in another it may mean recurrent health problems. How to decide? It's a matter of finesse gained through experience and intuition. The reader who can interpret the line accurately is the master reader. The line of liver is constantly changing: forming, reforming, dissolving, fading and even disappearing for some time and then returning. These changes correspond to states of health and vitality. Again, this stresses that readings are a 'here-now' experience.

When a person has the beginnings of a health problem, you will see a series of thin, diffused lines as opposed to one strong line. *See fig. 4.9*. This means a health problem is present and the individual is not paying enough attention to it.

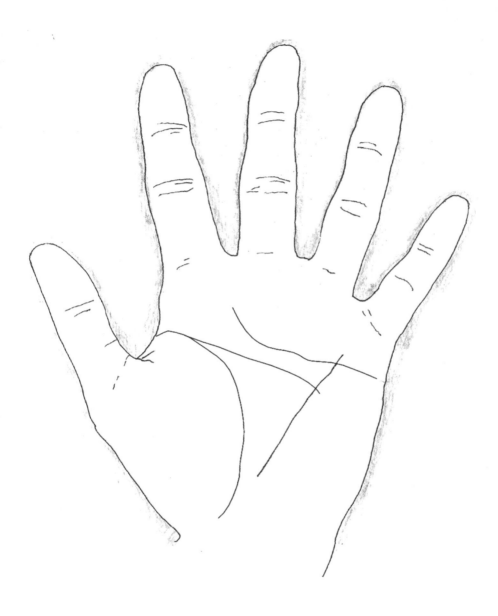

Fig. 4.8 Line of Liver

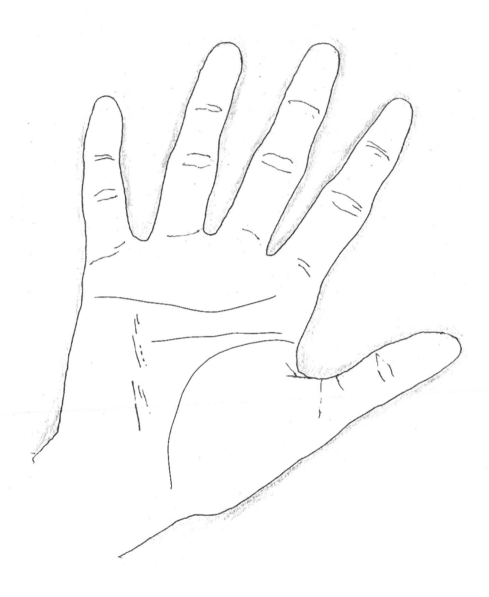

Fig. 4.9 Thin, Diffused Line of Liver

POISON LINE AND MARKINGS
ON THE LUNAR SIDE OF THE PALM
'Check It Out'

The poison line is a horizontal line beginning at the base of the palm on the lunar side extending for 1 to 2mm, and situated below the ending of the head line. This line is also known as the allergy line. *See fig. 4.10d.*

Very often someone with a poison line has an allergy to food. For many women this manifests as a weight problem. This line is very accurate. It means that an external substance which the body is being exposed to – either a certain food or something in the environment – is having an adverse effect upon the health of the person.

Further up the palm under the heart line there can be small horizontal lines. These mean digestive problems. There are lines when the gall bladder is chronically damaged or the liver is enlarged, usually from a bout of hepatitis. *See fig. 4.10a, b.*

Ridges and deep grooved lines and marks on the lunar side of the palm are a definite indication of chronic disease and sickness. *See fig. 4.10c.* These marking are extremely accurate; nearly all chronically ill persons have them.

Near the poison line there are other small horizontal lines and these are known as travel lines. *See fig. 4.10e.* However, now that travel is so quick and commonplace these lines are not as significant as they were 100 or 200 years ago, when taking a journey was a major event lasting many months or years.

You can make a good observation about health and how someone will die with the information obtained from:

- markings and weakness on the head and heart line
- loss of energy on life line by downward lines
- condition of the line of liver
- condition of the nails and skin

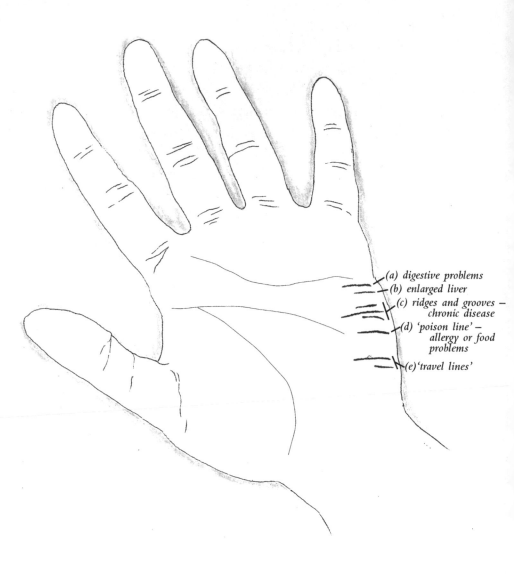

(a) *digestive problems*
(b) *enlarged liver*
(c) *ridges and grooves –*
       chronic disease
(d) *'poison line' –*
       allergy or food
       problems
(e) *'travel lines'*

Fig. 4.10 Markings on the Lunar Edge of the Palm

LINE OF MARS
'Someone Is Watching Over You'

The line of Mars runs alongside the life line, on the Venus side, for a varying distance. *See fig. 4.11.*

The line of Mars is a sister line to the life line, giving the person added strength and power. Funnily enough, I see it more often in women than in men. The line of Mars can appear and disappear as it is needed in a person's life. Often the line of Mars can absorb the energy from challenge, influence, worry and psychic lines, leaving the life line force intact and available for life. Without the Mars line(s), the individual would feel more tired and drained. There can be more than one line of Mars.

The line of Mars also signifies that the holder has a spiritual guide looking after him, protecting him from accidents and other dangers. I can confirm this in my hand and from my own life experience. One night I woke up from sleep because I felt someone slapping my face. I immediately saw that my blanket had caught fire from a candle left burning. I jumped up and put out the fire. I am sure that a spiritual guide had slapped my face to wake me up. There was no one else in the room at the time. Other people have told me similar stories.

MARRIAGE LINES
'Relationships'

Marriage lines are located under Mercury and above the heart line. They are usually straight little lines about 2–3mm in length. See *fig. 4.12.*

It is very hard to make predictions about marriage, and I've found these lines are not accurate on the subject – or about children, as is stated in many palmistry books. When there are small tiny lines rising from the marriage lines, it is supposed to mean children, but I've never found this to be true.

I feel that marriage lines have some connection with major relationships. A few

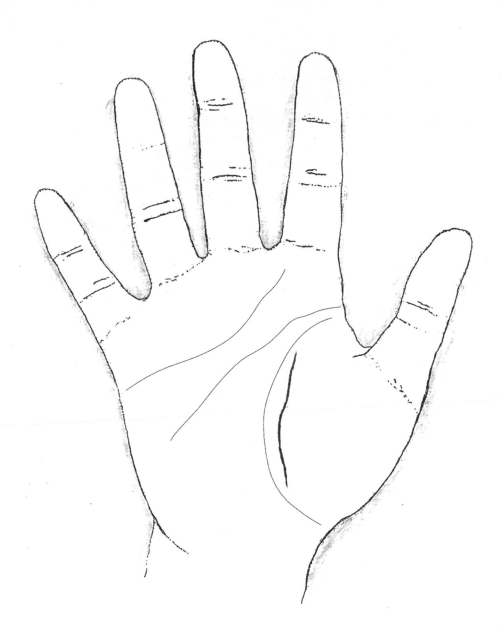

Fig. 4.11 Line of Mars

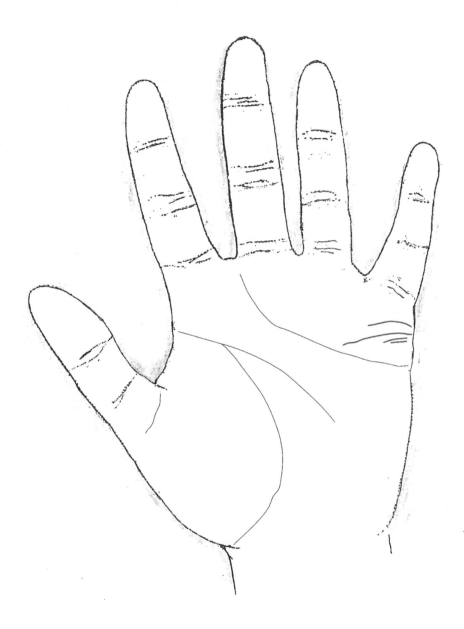

Fig. 4.12 Marriage Lines

straight marriage lines with no breaks mean the possibility of normal relationships. At least there is no blockage present. When a line slopes down towards the heart line, it can indicate that a major relationship will end with some hardship. This I have found to be true. Correlate this with the strength of the heart line and look to see if there are Xs between the heart and head line. The best solution is just to ask and probe when the subject asks about relationships. Let the answers arise from the subconscious. When two marriage lines are very close together it can mean relations with two people at the same time. I have seen this on a few occasions. If there are no marriage lines it does not mean the person will not have relationships or not get married. Again, look at other aspects to make comments about marriage.

Chapter 5

FURTHER ASPECTS
OF THE PALM

SPECIAL MARKINGS AND LINES

One general but very good rule applies when looking at markings on the hand: *vertical lines potentiate while horizontal lines are usually blocking. See fig. 5.1d,e.* This rule should always be used for interpreting special markings.

There can be all sorts of markings and unusual shapes on the palm. I suggest looking at other references that are more concerned with these markings. I present here only what I commonly observe in hands. My presentation is not complete, but if you follow the above rule you will be able to interpret most of the markings that can be present. If you follow this general rule you are more open to using intuition to discover what a marking means in a particular case. This is using logic to go to intuition.

Markings on the Palm
Two to three small, parallel, vertical lines under Mercury means success in business or talent in communications. *See fig. 5.1c.*

Under the Sun one solid vertical line shows the best creative channel. Many small lines are often seen and these mean that a creative channel is there but

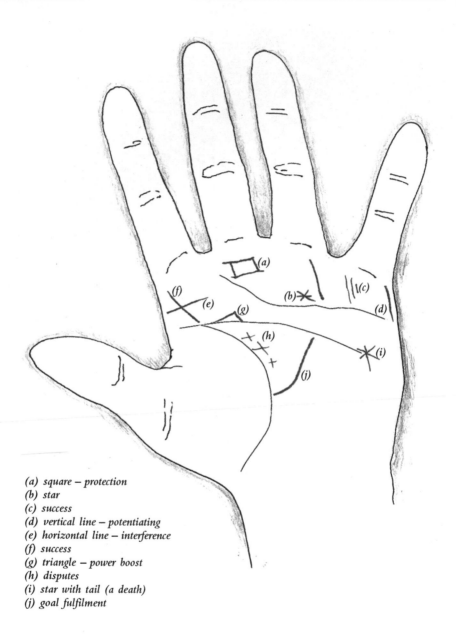

(a) square – protection
(b) star
(c) success
(d) vertical line – potentiating
(e) horizontal line – interference
(f) success
(g) triangle – power boost
(h) disputes
(i) star with tail (a death)
(j) goal fulfilment

Fig. 5.1 Markings on the Palm

needs development. With development the lines solidify and become one line.

Under Jupiter, look for lines rising from the life line. They indicate success. *See fig. 5.1f.* Horizontal lines on Jupiter mean interference. *See fig. 5.1e.*

Squares always mean protection. *See fig. 5.1a.*

Stars are a bit more difficult to interpret. Usually they are not good signs unless under the Sun. *See fig. 5.1b.* When a star with a tail is present, especially when the tail touches the head line, it means the death of an intimate friend or immediate family member. *See fig. 5.1i.* I've found stars with tails to be surprisingly accurate. In almost all cases the subject confirmed a death in the family or of a close friend, and in one instance I was able to predict the death of a family member.

When there is a line connecting the life line and head line exactly, it means fulfilment of a major goal at the point where it touches the life line. *See fig. 5.1j.*

Xs between the head and life line, at the beginning of their separation, mean litigation and family or land disputes. *See fig. 5.1h.*

Xs between the head and heart line mean hardships in major relationships.

Thin transparent trace lines

A palm contains the major and secondary lines and special markings. Along with these there are usually slight, fine, transparent lines which can be found anywhere along the palm. *See fig. 5.2.* These thin trace lines can be very interesting. Often they show activity on a subconscious level: new channels and directions forming, new connections brewing. You can watch these lines to see how they grow.

Sometimes these lines form precise patterns, interlacing with the primary and secondary lines. *See fig. 5.3.* This is a reflection of underlying patterns that the subject has generated, mostly from other lives. The patterns can be creative, psychological, and/or emotional.

Sometimes these underlying lines are as thick and as prominent as the major lines. They then represent special channels which have been created.

People with many web-like patterns are usually complex and can be highly strung. These persons have been evolving for some time. Their lives are complicated, because the life force travels through all these energy fields to reach

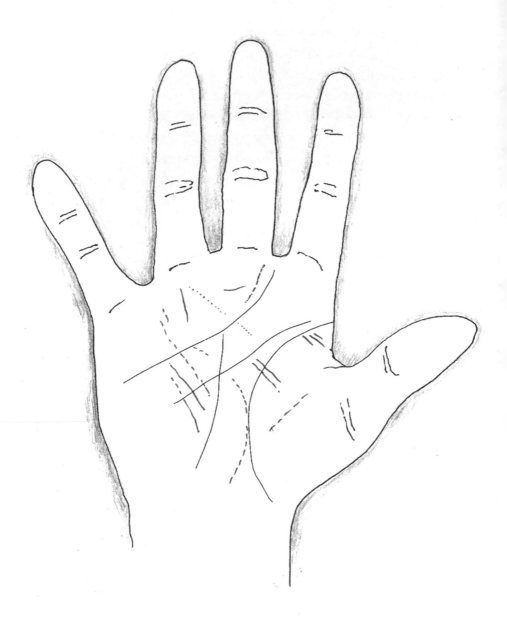

Fig. 5.2 Thin Trace Lines

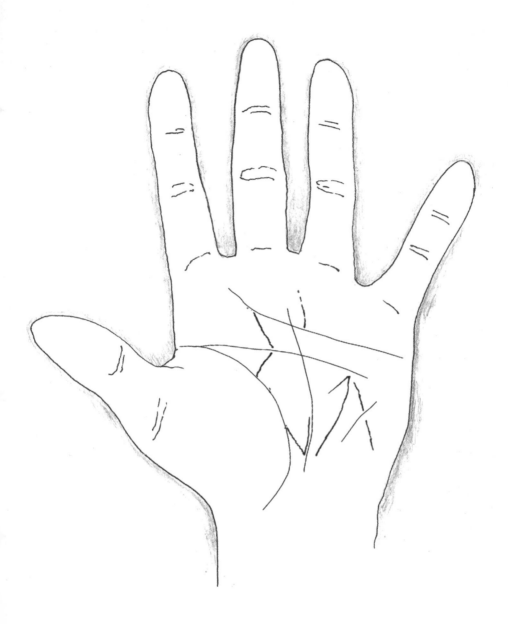

Fig. 5.3 Underlying Patterns

a conclusion. I always advise these types to simplify their lives and not form new creative channels – they are already inundated with them. We can become obsessed with creativity, it seems to be a natural impulse. Also, we are so conditioned to feel that to create is good and to do nothing is wrong. Creativity is fine, but up to a point.

It is beneficial for those with complex patterns to learn to be happy now, to simply be. They have gone as far as they can with doing and creativity and are now at the stage in their evolution where the discovery of their divine nature is much more important. Most of these people long for this discovery, although often they are not conscious of it.

Hands with many, many lines are hands of old souls. When you see such a hand in an 8-year-old child it is quite amazing. It is not so easy to give readings when there are so many lines, for many of the channels are ghost channels that are no longer utilised. But still the impressions are there. Don't try to analyse all the lines, just concentrate on the primary and secondary lines and whatever special lines catch your attention.

When there are many, many fine lines, the person can be highly strung and have nervous disorders, or is very often quite psychic with clairvoyant powers. In most cases you are dealing with a refined soul. At this stage of the person's evolution, the need for simplification is paramount. Further development and refinement would be only a hindrance.

Bracelets (rasceltes) – 'longevity'

Rings around the wrist just below the base of the palm are known as bracelets or rasceltes. *See fig. 5.4.* There can be up to three or four bracelets on the wrist. It is believed that the more bracelets present, the longer the life – but I have not confirmed this belief.

There is a correlation between the shape of the bracelet and childbirth. If the bracelet is well formed with no breaks, childbirth is favourable. Broken bracelets indicate childbirth difficulty. *See fig. 5.4a.*

You would imagine that the birth of a child would register quite significantly on the palm, since this is a major event. Why children remain so elusive baffles

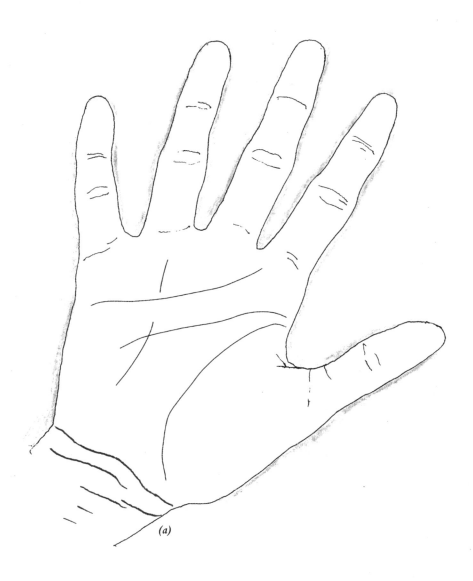

(a)

Fig. 5.4   Bracelets (Rasceltes)

me. The reason could be that I focus more on the spiritual side. Other palmists, especially Indian palmists and those who are more focused on family life, seem to be able to see children in the hand.

Recently I met a German palmist who examines the bracelets to determine the potential for having children, and by intuition decides the number of children. This is going from logic to intuition.

Simian line – 'the push to find the God within'

When the heart and head line are joined together it is called a simian line. Many variations are possible. *See fig. 5.5.* There can be one solid line, or there can be two lines joined together in some way.

The simian line gets its name from the fact that the same type of line is found in the palms of monkeys. The simian line is observed also in the hands of children with Down's syndrome, and it is one of the signs leading to and confirming this diagnosis.

A simian line means there is a particular aspect of karma to work through, usually something which presents difficulties for the person. Generally, to function in life effectively, it is easier to have a good clear separation between the emotional and mental body, since they flow in opposite directions and need space to act independently of each other.

Influences such as lines running down from the heart line or up from the head line usually have an inhibitory effect – mind is getting in the way of the emotional flow while emotions are colouring the actions of the mind.

When a simian line is present, it indicates that the emotional and mental bodies are joined together and exist as one. The heart can do nothing without the mind and the mind must consider the affairs of the heart.

For example, a person with a simian line can feel the utmost love for another person, but unless his mind is also saying yes the relationship will not work. The other must meet the criteria of his mind-set regarding what is acceptable and desirable in a relationship. If the mind is ignored, a disaster usually occurs, with one person getting hurt and the other feeling bad for causing that hurt.

Purity of the heart is difficult for someone with a simian line because the mind must be pure as well.

On the other hand, if the person is emotionally upset, it is very difficult for him to get on with life as far as logical action is concerned. Often, just the act of buying a banana cannot be performed because of emotional upset. It is not easy to live with this condition. It is said that the simian line is seen often in criminals and in people with a strong religious calling. Usually people with simian lines have both tendencies.

The key to transcending the joining of the emotional and mental body – and it must be transcended or the possessor will have a very difficult time – is, first, to understand his mixed nature and how to compensate for it and, second, meditation.

Through meditation, a simian-liner learns to witness himself, and to understand that he is something more than the body-mind mechanism. He begins to understand that he must listen to the mind and accept its presence when emotional issues are present, and vice versa. He learns that it is dangerous to enter into a relationship where there is love but the mind is saying no. Also, and very important, he learns to forgive himself when he cannot act like so-called 'normal' people, and to not get frustrated and be critical of himself. This kind of frustration and the involvement of strong emotions might account for why simian-liners resort to criminal acts.

A simian line is a very special message for the holder, telling him to go beyond the normal consciousness of ego identification and become the witness of mind-body phenomena.

A simian line is a strong push from existence to find the God within.

I have observed that all possessors of simian lines have within themselves some form of simplicity. Usually they have had in a past life some kind of mental disability or were simple minded, and in the current life some sense of this is still apparent. I have yet to find a person possessing a simian line where this is not the case. However, in this life the simplicity refers more to a natural simplicity than a mental disability.

In terms of evolutionary development, a simian line shows that the emotional body and mental body were joined in lower primates (monkeys) and have

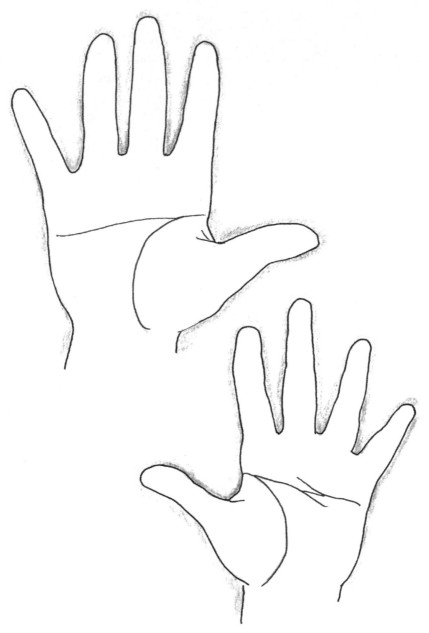

Fig. 5.5 Simian Line

separated in higher primates (man). Higher development then, is a clear separation of the mental and emotional bodies, and shows that the emotional body arose from the mental body. After all, emotions are nothing but thoughts with sensations attached to them.

Very rare markings

Ring of Solomon – 'wisdom'

The Ring of Solomon is rare: I've only met two people who have one. *See fig. 5.6a.* But, interestingly, I've started to develop one myself just in the last six months. The Ring of Solomon is a semicircular marking around the base of Jupiter – in either full or modified terms. The holder of a Ring of Solomon can give very wise and good advice to others, which King Solomon was noted for. However, it doesn't mean the holder can give wise advice to himself, and in the two cases that I have observed, this is true.

Mystic Cross

I have in fact never seen a Mystic Cross. *See fig. 5.6b.* It is a cross that is between the heart and head line, with the lines beginning and ending exactly on these two lines. This person is supposed to possess psychic talents.

Via Lascia

This line is found on the mount of Lunar. *See fig. 5.6c.* It indicates intuitive and psychic powers. Only just recently I found my first Via Lascia, and the person was indeed very sensitive and clairvoyant.

Triangle

A triangle formed by the life line, head line and line of liver is supposed to mean intuitive psychic powers. *See fig. 5.7.*

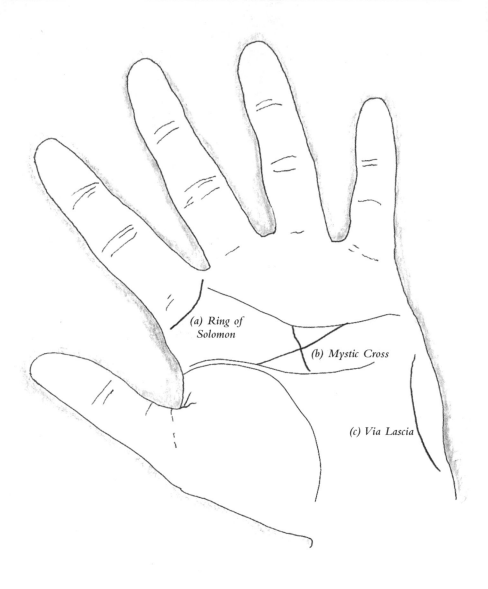

(a) Ring of Solomon

(b) Mystic Cross

(c) Via Lascia

Fig. 5.6 Rare Markings

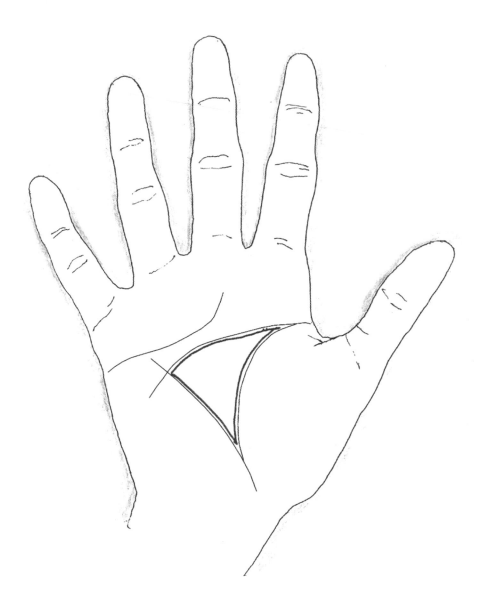

Fig. 5.7 Triangle

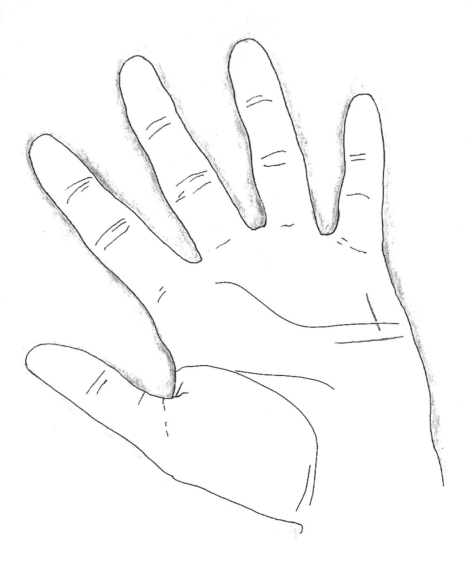

Fig. 5.8 Courage Lines Rising from the (-) Mount of Mars

Courage lines

Sometimes there can be a small line coming up from the (-) mount of Mars, travelling a short distance either horizontally or rising vertically and ending on a mount. *See fig. 5.8.* This line brings courage and fortitude to the mount and is a very special trait. It can sometimes be mistaken for a heart line or a second head line and often confuses palm readers.

Just recently I looked at the hands of a very interesting person – Mario Manseti, a spiritual teacher who is known as a 'Cosmic Master'. Some years ago he was stabbed in the heart. He died for eight minutes, and for the next year was blind and paralysed. But slowly he recovered. During this whole time Mario remained awake, and became fully conscious of his divine nature. He says that he returned to the body to help humanity, and ever since he has been healing and helping people.

Mario's hands reflect totally his story. In his left hand, he has a very strong head line running up to Jupiter. This head line shows the ability to influence large groups of people. In his right hand, his head line is very short, ending before Saturn. His life line ends in the middle of the palm, the area of the deep unconscious. A very strong, deep courage line runs horizontally across the palm. This line could almost be mistaken for a second head line.

These markings show that Mario's personality died and he is now a teacher and healer using the special channel of courage and fortitude. The energy and force of the courage line keep Mario in the body to do his work.

Spiritual seeker markings

In the middle of the base of the palm, where the Saturn line often originates, I have frequently observed a jumble of lines and crosses for which I could never find any reference in palmistry books. *See fig. 5.9.* I pondered over this for a long time until I began to correlate this bunch of lines with people who are spiritual seekers. I am quite sure this is true even though I cannot verify this with other authorities. Almost all spiritual seekers I know have these markings.

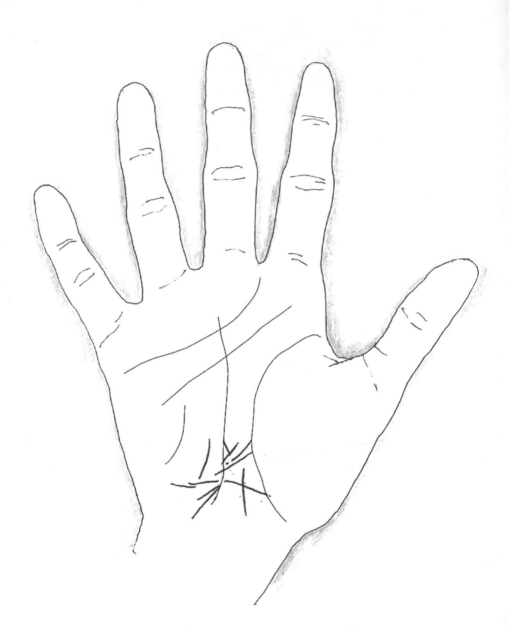

Fig. 5.9 Spiritual Seeker Markings

COMPARING THE TWO HANDS

Both the left and right hand need to be examined, for much information is obtained by comparing the hands. As a general rule (and it is a very general and loose rule), the passive hand (the left in a right-handed person) shows where someone is coming from – his past lives. The active hand shows what the person has done and accomplished or what he is in the process of accomplishing in this life.

The active hand must be determined at the beginning of the reading. This is done by discovering which hand reflects more accurately the subject's patterns. Begin the reading by assuming the person's hands follow the rule and only change if it becomes apparent during the course of the reading that the rule does not apply. The main point is to be flexible; the rule is a general guide and is not fixed.

Imprints and impressions, changing challenge and influence lines, and all the marks that accompany the life line can be imprinted in both hands, and sometimes more in the passive than the active hand. In this case, the rule has to be decided – the continuum might run from passive to active or vice versa. With left-handed people this is particularly so. Indeed, my conclusion from recent readings with left-handed people is that, more often than not, the right passive hand shows the active changes.

It is interesting when a decision has to be made for a person who is ambidextrous. The easiest way to determine which hand is the most active is to ascertain which one the person would use spontaneously in an emergency, even though this is not always the case. Usually some time is needed to discuss and decide on the active hand.

With all secondary and influence lines, both hands must be consulted, although usually one hand dominates. And do remember that the lines are always changing and reflect the condition of the individual in the here and now.

The passive hand reflects the state of evolution up until birth, while the active hand reflects changes in evolution as a result of the present life. If a baby is born with differences between the hands, it means that the process of change that was taking place in the last life is continuing in the current life.

Some continuum can be observed with the hands. When the major lines are basically the same in both hands, it means a continuation of the status quo, with no major transitions occurring. If these lines are affected, the subject is continuing with issues that have been occurring for some time in other lives. Either more time is needed to resolve these issues, or he is avoiding them. The latter occurs when an issue is prominent in the person's consciousness, or lack of consciousness.

When the lines are developed, a continuum poses no problem, and in fact it is good that the lines remain the same. For example, with a full heart line there is no need for further development – stability has been achieved. Now the subject can go on to higher realms of evolution.

At any point in evolution, we can become enlightened. We don't need to reach an end point to realise our own self. I have looked at the hands of at least two enlightened beings, and in both there were still many affected lines and issues. And I could see that these issues were also going on in their lives. However (and it's a big however), these two enlightened beings were not identified with the issues; they were living beyond, in the grace of higher consciousness. When I first looked at the hands of Papaji (my spiritual master), I was shocked and couldn't believe what was present. Then I saw that what Papaji had done was simply get off the train, leaving all the baggage behind. The train goes on with the baggage but there is no Papaji on the train.

Now we come to the situation where there is a change in one or more of the major lines from one hand to the other. Of course, a change means a transition, a time of active growth, or a withdrawal (if the line is affected). If all the major lines show changes, a person will be in an extreme state of flux. He may feel quite confused, not knowing where to put his feet or hang his hat. The old and new both have force. If the person has achieved some consciousness, it can mean a life of profound growth and enlightenment. To experience the beyond, chaos is often needed to overcome the confinements of evolution. It is important to show the subject the changes he is undergoing. Understanding can be very helpful to such a person. Since both the new and old modes are present and still operating, he might as well take a leap and choose the new mode when confusion and indecision occur.

If only one line is showing change there is more stability to handle the transition. And if the person has achieved some development, he may be able to utilise both old and new modes. Sometimes, it is not that the old channel is deficient but the fact that a change is needed so the person can learn or see aspects of himself and the world in a new way. Therefore, utilisation of both channels can be beneficial. Take, for example, the case of a person who has an intuitive head line in the left hand and a practical head line in the right hand. One explanation for this is that the person has become too focused on his intuitive side and now needs to attain balance by focusing more on the outer, physical world. Although change is needed, the person can still utilise the intuitive mental channel in his left hand when necessary. Most people don't even know that they can access different channels.

CHANGES IN THE MAJOR LINES

Understanding the mechanics of the body-mind machine can greatly help alleviate suffering. Changes in the major lines mean there is desire within the person for change. The person may or may not be conscious of this desire to change. If he is conscious of it, the striving and change is welcomed; if not the striving can be misunderstood and resisted, leading to suffering and blame.

There are cases when one or more major lines retract, becoming smaller and fainter. There can be several reasons for this: a hostile environment, dramatic early-life events, or past-life karma. Usually the person feels that he has shut down, and has a subconscious memory of having been more open.

For whatever reason, a channel can shut down and operate at a lower level. This retraction is needed sometimes for further growth. With some people it is good to encourage expansion and stimulation of the affected channel, and with others I find it is better to advise caution and protection. I once examined the hand of a small girl whose major lines were all retracting. She was born to a Western woman and an Indian man. The family lived in India, where to a large extent women's growth and freedom are suppressed. This environment was reflected in the retracted lines of her hands. When the family asked me whether they should live in India or the West, I replied that it would be better for the girl to live in the West where there is more freedom of expression. The family has since returned to England. It would be interesting to see the hand of the girl now.

Injuries and scars on the hand

Injuries on the palm confuse and distort the picture. When there are scars and operations, I generally discount the meanings of the lines in those areas.

COMPARISON OF THE PRIMARY AND SECONDARY LINES

This is an important section because it concerns the reason(s) why a person incarnates into a particular birth. It identifies the main driving force, the one that sustains life and gives sustenance.

I examine the hand to discover which line or lines appear to be the most prominent and strong. The dominant line(s) gives clues concerning the why and how of incarnation. There is not a hard-and-fast rule for which hand to examine – usually it is the dominant hand, but at times the passive hand also gives clues. When examining the hands, follow what catches your eye, since both hands can contain valid information.

When the Saturn line is very strong, it means the person has a fixed destiny from which he cannot waver. The sole reason for his incarnation is the playing out and completion of the story.

When the life line is weak, the person is a part of someone else's story. Very often we incarnate for other souls. In fact, a weak life line is a good sign because it shows that further development of the personal 'I' is not important and the possibility of enlightenment is very close. It can mean the end of the ego story.

When the life line is strong the destiny story is more about the person's own growth and evolution. When the life line is the strongest and the dominant line, the story of the current life is most important, and it may or may not have a fixed destiny.

When the head line is dominant, it is mental power that sustains the life and gives sustenance. Usually there is a need to complete an action, for the head line is masculine. We can live without a life line but not without a head line.

When the heart line is prominent, the main reason for life is love, and it is love that keeps the person alive and moving. When love is withdrawn, he will die, as if from a broken heart.

There are instances when a Saturn line starting in the lunar area is the strongest line. This means the person is powered by the merits of his past spiritual practices and experiences – so much so that this is the only source that keeps him alive. It could mean the soul incarnated to help others or teach.

Chapter 6

GIVING A READING

TO GIVE IS DIVINE

We come now to the most challenging but the most rewarding section of the book.

Giving a reading is a mystery, a dive into the miraculous, into the unknown; a process of going from the logical to the intuitive and from the intuitive to the logical. To go from the logical to the intuitive means using observed known facts to say something beyond facts or logic – in other words, using facts as stepping stones to jump into the waters of intuition.

For example, once I was giving a reading to a French woman. In her hand there was a small downward line running near the beginning of the life line. I know that this line means additional life force, and because it is a downward line I know it is an affected line. And it just came to me suddenly and I said, 'Oh, you have a twin brother and there was some trouble with him.' She said, 'Yes, he died, and it was a horror story for me.'

You look, examine the indications and then all of a sudden you have an intuitive flash of interpretation, which is more than just the sum of the logical parts.

The reverse can happen as well. Flashes occur and then you find evidence in the hand to support the intuition.

All this is not something that can really be taught. You can be led to the edge of the cliff, but jumping off is up to you. Everything in this section is like a finger pointing you to the cliff, leading and helping, but you must be the one to jump. This jump does require some inborn ability to give readings, but if you are reading this book then most likely that talent is already there.

The knowledge and practice of palmistry will take some time. Don't expect to become a master of it in less than seven years. During this time you are a student, so buy as many books as you can and study them. There is useful information in all of them, but there is also a lot of false information, read in one book and copied into another without verification. After reading, start looking at palms; find out what is true and begin to accumulate your own store of knowledge.

Detailed analysis of your own palm is very useful, because you know what your traits are. Make palmistry a hobby and impress your friends at the same time. Remember, with a limited range of vocabulary you can still give a reading even if you are a student. And if you lose interest, don't worry; you will come back to it.

After learning a sufficient amount of meanings and having spent time analysing your own hand, you will be ready to look at other hands to give readings. Start by examining people's hands and discussing whether the lines reflect the person's reputed characteristics, without giving a reading.

When you feel you are ready to give a reading, have the person sit in front of you and ask him to give you his hands to look at. Take the hands and at first just hold them, allowing a general impression to come to you. For example, there may be something elegant about the hand. The lines and shape of the palm can be beautiful, with an intricate and pleasing design. Or the opposite may be the case: the major lines may be crossed by many secondary lines so that the palm resembles a battlefield.

Look first at the shape of the hands and lines as a whole, as a pattern. This can provide a good insight before you start to look at details. Take your time. Look over the hand and fingers without making judgements, allowing impressions to enter into your consciousness. Then slowly start taking in details of the shape, size and strength of the hands, going over everything from the checklist on page 133. Once you have looked everything over, compare both hands for differences. When you feel ready you can begin to speak. Remember, you don't have to reveal everything about every little line in the hand.

Often many pictures and images will come and you will find many interesting points to make, and at other times nothing will come and you will not know what to say or how to begin. In this case, I ask the person what it is that he wants to know, and this very often breaks the ice. I find that the openness of the subject is extremely important in regard to how insightful the reading is. When the subject openly tells you what he wants to know, it is much easier to go deeper with him into unravelling the subconscious and discovering underlying motives and tendencies.

Another method I use to begin a reading is to concentrate on the aspects that catch my attention and seem to be the major story of the subject. I can limit a reading to these aspects and don't feel that I have to give a complete reading, telling what every line means. Sometimes it is appropriate to tell all and at other times it is better to focus on one issue.

When a person comes for a reading he is seeking some form of communication that will result in a greater understanding of himself. It doesn't matter how that happens or how much information is given.

Sometimes I start the reading by showing the subject where the lines are and what they represent, and then let the reading progress from there. People with straight head lines need to see proof, so I show them exactly where on the palm I base my statements. This relaxes them and they get more into the reading. And I try to take them through the process of my deductions.

People with intuitive head lines don't require such detailed proof, but they like you to say something intuitive. People with slightly curved head lines like the psychoanalytical approach. Often I adjust my reading to bring the subject into more openness and trust.

I try not to judge what I say. Sometimes I have nothing but negative points to tell and sometimes the opposite. *You have to trust that what you are saying is what the person needs to hear.* And when it isn't, usually you can immediately sense this. I guess it is good to be ready to admit you are wrong, even if it puts you in a bad light. And if you don't know something, just say you don't know.

Remember, we can never see the whole picture. We are always looking through the peephole. Palmistry exists as a totality, but our perceptions are limited. And also, the person doesn't need to know everything.

Those who want to know everything are the greedy types. Usually their fingers have first and second phalanges that are thick and/or long, with the third phalange tapering to a point, as with psychic fingers. I always have the impression of a pig's fingers. This is a personal judgement, but it always turns out that these people ask, 'When I will get this or have that?'

When I asked a subject what he wanted to know and he replied, 'Nothing, I am just curious about the lines', I used to accept this and give a general reading. Usually the person wanted confirmation of my competence. Now that I no longer worry about a subject's judgements, I continue to probe, telling him that the more focused and specific he is the deeper we will be able to go. I can enjoy showing my talents with palmistry, but that is not the point. The point is to help the person understand maybe just one little point, or to clarify one tiny aspect of his life.

There are a few markings on the palm that are always correct – for example, the early part of the life line showing early childhood, and the early part of the heart line showing the mother's relationship with the child. I believe what the palm tells me about these areas even if the subject tells me the exact opposite. And always at some point the subject begins to admit something about himself, usually in an off-hand statement when he is not thinking about what he is saying. These types of readings I find to be the most exhausting, although it is rewarding when the ice finally breaks.

With some readings nothing happens. This cannot be helped.

MAKING AN EXAMINATION

Always try to hold both hands as much as possible during the entire reading. Make a systematic examination following the checklist below. Just try to observe without making conclusions until you have finished your examination. The meanings of the lines and markings are complete in themselves. However, because we exist as a functioning, integrated unit, the lines (channels) modify each other. For example, a weak thumb, which channels logic and willpower, can neutralise a strong head line. So when giving a reading you must examine all factors before making a conclusion. Give yourself a moment to reflect before you begin.

Checklist

1 Examine the shape of the hand:
- type of hand – fire, water, earth or air
- long or short fingers
- low- or high set thumb
- length of thumb
- the angle of spread between Jupiter and thumb

2 Examine the shape of the fingers:
- straight or crooked
- short or long
- relationship to other fingers
- direction of flow of energy through fingers
- knots
- flexibility (check by bending back fingertips)
- fingertip types
- fingerprints
- length and relationship of the phalanges to each other and to the palm

3 Feel the hand to determine if the palm is soft, elastic or firm. Look at the colour of the skin and check the nails.

4 Examine the lines in detail.
i Note the general types of lines and if and where there are changes in the hand.
ii Determine the passive and active hands.
iii Study the heart line:

- Which type is it?
- Check beginning of line.
- Look for breaks, gaps, etc.
- Is it high or low set?

iv Study the life line:
- Examine it from beginning to end, noting its strengths and weaknesses.
- Where and how does it begin?
- Where and how does it end?
- Look for breaks, gaps, etc. and any upward or downward lines coming to and from the line.
- Are there challenge and influence lines?

v Study the head line:
- Which type is it?
- Examine it from beginning to end. Is it a strong line, red in colour, or is it pale and faint? Does the thickness vary?
- Are there breaks, islands, chains or gaps? Is the line wavy or straight? Are there any markings on the line?
- Look at its relationship to the life line and the heart line – is it close or at some distance from them?

5 Examine the mounts:
- Ascertain which one is dominant and which ones are developed or recessed.
- Check if the mount is directly under the finger or a little askew.
- Look for special markings.

6 Examine the secondary lines:
- Saturn
- Sun
- Mercury
- Mars

7   Check for special markings:
- on Mars
- on side of palm
- poison lines
- bracelets

8   Check for:
- thin trace lines
- challenge and influence lines on rest of the palm

Keep going back and forth comparing both hands. Look for changes between the palms.

Take some time to look at the health indicators. Ask about the person's health.

When you are satisfied, you can begin the reading. Continue to hold the hands if possible.

A good way to begin is to tell the subject what types of lines he has and go on from there. Try to show him what you see in the palm, although you don't have to do so all at once.

Don't be afraid to ask questions to clarify the meaning of lines, because the lines or markings can have several meanings.

Get the person to share. For example, if you see markings on the (+) Mars, which can mean father trouble, ask about the father and the subject's relationship with him. Do the same with the mother if you see markings on the beginning of the heart line.

Find out what the subject needs in order to feel satisfied with the reading. In fact, this is another good way to begin. Ask the person what exactly it is he needs to know to feel satisfied.

Each reading will be different. Some readings are exciting and provide great insights, others are boring and reveal no connections at all. When this happens, don't worry; nothing fits perfectly and there are always exceptions to the rules.

As you get into the reading, keep talking and keep examining the hands. You will find new lines and keep seeing different aspects. Try to keep the subject involved. Further insights will surface as the reading goes on.

Giving a reading is a mystery. Seeing all the lines and markings will give you some intuitive sense about the subject – a sense you might not even be able to translate into words. Accept that you can't describe everything you see.

When giving a reading you will be going from logic to intuition and vice versa. What does this mean? This means that you will be observing the logical and scientific and staying in the known meanings of the lines, and then at some point you will have an intuitive feeling or insight.

On the other hand, an intuitive sense may be present which is verified by the logical meanings of the lines. For example, you may have a sense that the person does not love himself and then notice indications on the hand that this is correct.

You will discover what your talents are and how to use them as you go along. The fact that you are reading this means some talent is there.

Each person seems to have certain threads (tendencies) that run through life – problems with relationships, for example. Now, how that manifests in the person's life and what the specifics of the story are, is not always easy to tell, so it is best just to ask. The more information a person gives you the better. Don't waste time trying to prove yourself. Ask the person what he wants to know and what would satisfy him. It is amazing how deep and meaningful a reading can be when the subject is open; when he genuinely wants answers and is not just wanting to see if the reader is psychic or not. However, sometimes we need to play that game when first giving readings. It also satisfies our own egos!

I am not including a sample reading, because I do not want you to develop a fixed idea of what a reading should be like.

Don't expect to become an expert in one day. Even if you can identify all the meanings of the lines you may not be able to interpret them. For example, you may know that someone has an intuitive head line, but what does that imply?

It is best to let the imagination flow. See if a story happens. This is going from the logical to the intuitive.

Sessions usually just end when everyone has had enough. Ask one more time if there are any more questions.

You will walk away with a different feeling after each reading. You can feel charged or drained. Some readings are really fun and others are hard work. Most important, though, is the effect the reading has on the person.

If possible, try to connect with the person again by saying that he is free to contact you if any questions come up later.

Learning to read the palm never ends, and you will find yourself getting better and better as the scope of your knowledge, intuition and practical experience increases.

FURTHER READING

Cheiro, *Palmistry: the Language of the Hand,* Random House, New York, 1999. New edition of the work first published in 1894 as *Cheiro's Language of the Hand.*

The Benham Book of Palmistry: A Practical Treatise on the Laws of Scientific Hand Reading, Newcastle Publishing Co., 1989. New edition of W.G. Benham's *Laws of Scientific Hand Reading,* first published in 1900.

Comte C. De Saint-Germain, *The Study of Palmistry for Professional Purposes and Advanced Purposes,* Kessinger Publishing Co., 1997. Reprint of 1897 edition.

Bharat welcomes questions from readers about the practice of palmistry and the meaning of lines. His e-mail address is: ombharatji@aol.com

INDEX